UNLEASH THE Best You

365
INSPIRATIONS AND ACTIONABLE
TIPS TO TRANSFORM
YOUR LIFE

MOUSTAFA KADOUS

Table of Contents

DEDICATION

– II –

YOUR JOURNEY BEGINS

– VI –

Chapter 1

ACTIONS

– 1 –

Chapter 2

OVERCOME BARRIERS & LIMITING BELIEFS

– 51 –

Chapter 3

INSPIRATION & MOTIVATION

– 87 –

Chapter 4

INNER STRENGTH & CONFIDENCE

– 113 –

Chapter 5

FORGIVENESS, LETTING GO, & BALANCE

– 135 –

Chapter 6

PERSISTENCE

– 163 –

Chapter 7
PLANS AND VISUALIZATION

– 187 –

Chapter 8
BELIEFS & MINDSET

– 215 –

Chapter 9
SUCCESS

– 247 –

Chapter 10
FOCUS

– 285 –

Chapter 11
HONESTY AND DREAMS FOR THE FUTURE

– 329 –

Chapter 12
SELF-CARE AND SELF-DEVELOPMENT

– 351 –

YOUR JOURNEY CONTINUES.

– 389 –

About the Author

– 390 –

DEDICATION

To my wife and children for their love and belief in me, their sacrifices and endless encouragement through words and actions. I LOVE YOU.

To my amazing readers who will invest their time to read this book and get the best out of it — to become the best they can be.

Without you, my dreams will remain unfulfilled.

YOUR JOURNEY BEGINS

Who are you?

This is the most important question you need to ask yourself — and then discover the answer.

What the world sees when they look at you is not your whole story; it may even be the wrong story. Based on my life's many ups and downs, I've learned, however, that our external reality ends up aligning with our authentic inner self.

So, create your reality and unlock your best you.

While you can't predict what's going to happen in life, you can choose to live an authentic life that leads to the life you desire and one that comfortably aligns with your intentions. Now is the time to discover your place, your calling, and the truth about "who you are."

If you are like many people, becoming an all-round better person is a constant and growing challenge. It's often a struggle to stay motivated and focused 365 days a year whether at work, home, or school, especially on Monday mornings. And, life only gets harder the moment you decide to embrace the easy life and avoid the challenges of life.

That's why I wrote this book of inspirations, reflections, and actions. It's about inspiring you with a thought, reflecting upon what it means to you and for you. Then, it's up to you to act on it. How will you embody the message, or share it, or change what you do today to be a better person, to improve your life, to move forward with purpose throughout your day?

By taking a few moments each day with this book, I believe you can discover how to unlock the best in you, and be prepared to confidently navigate anything and everything about life.

I hope that my book gives you the right nudge to grab the bull of life by its horns to accomplish your life goals.

Always remember:

> Just because we swept the floor once doesn't mean the floor will remain clean permanently. We must sweep every day the dust comes back
>
> Ryan Holiday

Unlocking the best version of you is like sweeping the floor. You must do it every day. Grab the broomstick and sweep to keep the dust from coming back. Let's get started. Your dreams are waiting for you.

Chapter One

ACTIONS

> *If you will pump long enough, hard enough, and enthusiastically enough sooner or later, the effort will bring forth the reward.*
>
> Zig Ziglar

1 | Increase Your Actions; Never Reduce Your Targets

> *When you start rethinking your targets, making up excuses, and letting yourself off the hook, you are giving up on your dreams!*
>
> *Grant Cardone*

Instead of reading four books per month to sharpen your selling skills, you're tempted to reduce it to two or one just in case. However, it doesn't mean you should set unrealistic targets which can make you give up altogether.

That just sets a precedent to choose the easy way out. Then, the next time you feel challenged, you will tend to reduce your goals. Consequently, you might never explore your actual limits.

When you're in doubt, always say to yourself, "I prefer to fall short of meeting my original goals than succeed because I cut them by half". Do whatever is necessary to reach your target.

Measure Your Real Decisions | 2

> *A real decision is measured by the new action you have taken. Without action, you haven't truly made a decision.*

Tony Robbins

Until you take a real-world action that reflects your decision, don't conclude that you've decided yet. For example, suppose you've chosen to make changes to your nutritional habits. Until you prepare a healthy meal, you haven't made that decision yet. The moment you take a real-world action and can no longer back out easily is the moment your decision becomes real.

3 | There Is No Such Thing as the Perfect Time

> *If we wait until we're ready, we'll be waiting for the rest of our lives.*
>
> *Lemony Snicket*

You will perform more meaningful work every day once you acknowledge that there is never a perfect time for you to take action on anything. Instead of thinking far into the future, utilize the resources currently available to you and experience the magic of creativity.

Act despite the self-criticism and self-doubt; bring that idea to life now.

Specific Outcomes | 4

> *You may never know what results come of your actions, but if you do nothing, there will be no results.*

Mahatma Gandhi

Put your knowledge and skills to practical use. It's good to have skills, resources, connections, and capabilities. But, it's more fulfilling when you can deploy them in the service of a worthy goal. Put your love and care for what matters to you into actions that create specific outcomes.

When you combine your skills with purpose, you will discover that you can make a whole lot of difference in your life and in the lives of others.

5 | Release All Negative Emotions

> *Negative emotions have an important role to play in a happy life; they're big, flashing signs that something needs to change.*
>
> *Gretchen Rubin*

It can be hard to make decisions that align with your true feelings when you're angry or sad. Instead of feeling upset, annoyed, or frustrated, you need to find proper ways to release your negative emotions and make your situations a bit better. Then, you can enjoy your present, be more productive, and reach your goals.

Deep breathing, journaling, physical exercise, deep sleep, and meditation are ways you can release all your negative emotions.

Act on Quick Tasks Immediately | 6

> Now and too late are the only two times in life. I choose Now every time.

Moustafa Kadous

It is quite easy to put off quick tasks because they are easy and fast to do. If you don't do them immediately, these quick tasks accumulate and turn into a time-consuming project.

Furthermore, putting off that quick task because you don't feel like doing it immediately can lead to a habit of procrastination.

Instead of postponing that quick task that can take less than 10 minutes, do it immediately.

7 | Don't Wait to be Saved

> *What saves a man is to take a step. Then another step.*

Antoine de Saint-Exupery

It is easy to get stuck to the belief that someone or something must save you before you can make any accomplishment. Unless you find the right coach, you won't start exercising. Why not put on your sneakers and go for a walk. It beats sitting and wishing.

Unless the perfect, flawless person appears in your life, you won't start a long-term relationship.

Why not accept that nobody is perfect (which is a fact by the way) and embrace their positive traits and flaws. You only need to identify the flaws you can live with.

You must walk your path without waiting to be saved. You can use other people's resources, but don't use them as crutches.

Stop Worrying About What's Beyond Your Control | 8

> *Worrying about anything, especially what you can't control, won't bring it to reality.*

Moustafa Kadous

While you can't control many things that happen in life, you can determine what you can control.
Replaying conversations over and over or imagining catastrophic outcomes won't solve the problem. Productive thinking is the best solution.

Stop and ask yourself whether your thoughts are productive. If it is productive, keep along that channel of thought and keep brainstorming solutions. If not, change your brain's thought patterns.

First, get up and do something different for a few minutes. Then, come back to focus your brain on productive measures.

9 | Find Opportunities Amid the Chaos

> *Opportunity is missed by most people because it is dressed in overalls and looks like work.*
>
> Thomas A. Edison

You might struggle to have logical thoughts in chaos, and that's understandable. But you might discover new opportunities in the chaos by examining the situation without any emotion clouding your judgment. Suppose one "cheat" meal turns into a week-long binge. Instead of concluding that everything is lost and giving up, use it as an opportunity to identify what made you eat it and find other ways to satisfy your junk food cravings without eating it.

Identify the opportunities in chaos and the benefits might last for a lifetime.

You Are Ready | 10

> *The greatest use of life is to spend it for something that will outlast it.*

William James

You can create real value in unlimited ways. You are in the right moment, and you are in an ideal place to move forward. So, delight yourself with the possibilities and get creative.

Don't doubt it, you can make it happen because you are ready to be your best and live your best.

Share your knowledge with the world and as that beauty keeps unfolding, you will bask in the joy of your discovery.

11 | Build on Your New Experiences

> *A mind that is stretched by a new experience can never go back to its old dimensions.*
>
> *Oliver Wendell Holmes Jr.*

At some level, there is a connection among all fields of knowledge when we delve deeper and deeper into each field. Since you can often apply big ideas to general life, you should have a basic understanding of the key concepts of important disciplines such as history, mathematics, physics, biology, psychology, and engineering.

Let's take personal growth. No one wants to grow at a fixed rate. I don't, and you shouldn't. Your growth rate will increase at an alarming pace when you constantly build on your new experiences.

With a deliberate focus on the basics, strive to educate yourself in various fields. Then, apply these basic principles to real-world situations. Even if you don't always find the application, self-education alone is an important part of unlocking the best you.

Decisions and Consequences | 12

> *My actions are my only true belongings. I cannot escape the consequences of my actions. My actions are the ground on which I stand.*

Thich Nhat Hanh

Always consider the first-order and second-order consequences. For instance, if you choose to skip a workout, the first-order consequence is that you can relax and do something more pleasant. The second-order consequence is that you've altered your routine. As a result, you are gradually returning to your old, unfit self.

No matter how small, there is more to each decision you make than the way it makes you feel immediately by considering second-order consequences, you will discern between meaningless immediate gratification and the power in delaying rewards for a better outcome in the future.

13 | Analysis Paralysis Is Real

> *Analysis paralysis occurs when you overthink and underwork.*
>
> Orrin Woodward

When you overthink a situation to the extent of not taking action, then you have analysis paralysis. Like driving a car in foggy weather, you can work on your objectives even with limited knowledge.

If you tend to overcomplicate and overanalyze things, find a "good enough" answer to one vital question instead of searching for the perfect answer for everything.

Commit to a Small, Consistent Act of Self-Control | 14

> *The man who moves a mountain begins by carrying away small stones.*

Confucius

Never disregard the power of small efforts. When you repeat some of these small efforts, it can lead to immense personal changes since you will now be more mindful of your daily actions.

You develop more mindfulness and become a better version of yourself by pausing yourself intermittently throughout the day to control your small behaviors.

Even when you're strapped for time, consider adding these little exercises to your daily routine:
- Keep a journal of new ideas that can improve you.
- Don't curse unless you have taken a 5-minute pause.
- Work with your back straight.

15 | Set a New Challenge

> *Set new challenges for yourself. It keeps your zest for life alive.*

Tracy Todd

If you don't have any important long-term goals to achieve, then you will catch yourself wandering, feeling you have no purpose, and asking yourself the purpose of life. Celebrate the achievement of your important goals. Then, set a new challenge within a couple of weeks of achieving that important long-term goal.

Be sure you have secondary goals or a "waiting list" of goals. Whenever you can't come up with a new primary goal after accomplishing your primary goal, you can make your secondary goals your new objective.

Create Your Path in Life | 16

> Make your way, forget about people, act in your style. But never let the people forget you.

Ketan

You must make the journey and choose your life's direction even when others point the way or give you their assistance and advice. No one can give you everything you desire no matter their generosity or good-heartedness. The reward of creating your achievements far exceeds any other reward.

Make the commitment and the effort to create your own beautiful path in life.

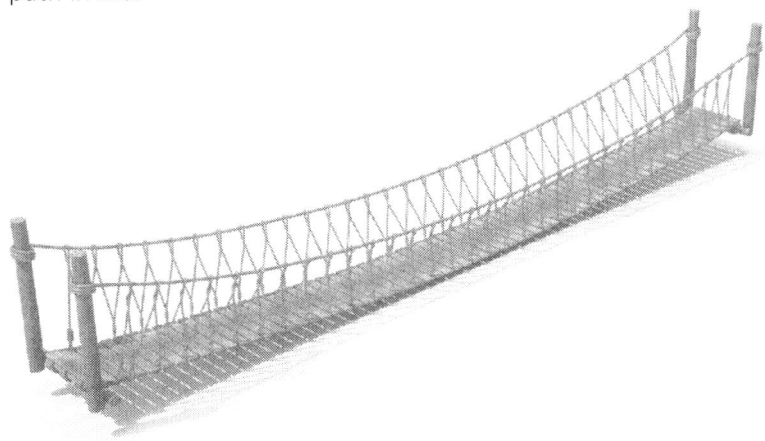

17 | Give Yourself Less Time to Worry About the Changes

> They always say time changes things, but you have to change them yourself.
>
> *Andy Warhol*

Whenever you are facing a big change in life, it is normal to hesitate; you will be facing the unknown which can be very scary. The best way to prevent anxiety from growing is by taking the plunge as quickly as possible. Rather than wait, you will resolve the situation more effectively.

You Are the Result of Your Actions

> *your thoughts, your words and your actions created the life you are living. you create your results - no one else.*

Lary Winget

Though you control the actions you take or don't take, your actions also control you in the long term because they determine the person you'll become. So, always ask yourself what your future self would do or not do before making a decision. Beyond the immediate consequences, consider each of your actions as a building block of a new you.

19 | Shake Yourself Out of Inaction

> *I never worry about action, but only about inaction.*
>
> *Winston Churchill*

Once in a while, imagine that you have a few months to live and choose a task from your bucket list. Apart from discovering your true priorities, it serves as a powerful boost to act immediately. While it is awful to think about death, it can be your inspiration to shake you out of inaction.

Since you are still alive and kicking, why not make your dreams a reality, one after the other.

Stop the procrastination now!

Make That Decision | 20

> *Your life changes the moment you make a new, congruent and committed decision.*

Tony Robbins

If you are afraid you will make the wrong decision, then you are constantly expecting failure. You put yourself in a negative mindset because of problems that might never happen when you delay or avoid making the decision.

It's only through action that you can succeed and accomplish your goals. But you must make an active decision before you can take action.

So, make that decision and take action. If your decision is wrong, you'll learn what you need to do and correct it.

21 | The Long-Term Consequences of Your Decisions

Every choice you make has a result.

Zig Ziglar

If there were no consequences to your actions, then you wouldn't make any tangible accomplishments. And, you wouldn't have any basis to control the circumstances of your life. You do gain the power to determine the consequences of your life by taking responsibility for such consequences.

Carefully analyze the effect of each decision you make before making such decisions. Then, you can create the results you desire.

Make Important Decisions When You Are Less Emotional | 22

> *When you fuel your positive thoughts with positive emotions, they will change your life.*

Moustafa Kadous

I give myself at least a day to think about big purchases, and it doesn't matter whether the purchase is over the phone or in person. I suggest that you do likewise and apply it when setting big goals.

Setting goals when you're 'under the influence' might make you overestimate your abilities and set goals that you can't reach.

23 | For Every Cause, There Is a Definite Effect

> *Every cause produces more than one effect.*
>
> *Herbert Spencer*

Through your thoughts, behaviors, and actions, you create specific effects that manifest and create your life the way you know it.

If you are not satisfied with the current effects, then you need to change the causes that created them.

This can involve changing your actions by transforming your thoughts.

Turn Your Weaknesses to Strength | 24

Sometimes, you need the struggle to find your greatest strengths.

Moustafa Kadous

An important step to get beyond your weakness is to admit that you have it. Once you have clarity about the weakness, you will develop effective ways to work on it. There is a strength with which you can replace each of your weaknesses because you can always learn a valuable lesson from your weakness.

Have the courage to face your weakness and use the factors that work against you to propel you forward. Identify the opportunities from your weakness.

25 | Adopt a New Perspective

> *If you don't like something, change it; if you can't change it, change the way you think about it.*
>
> Mary Engelbreit

If you are disappointed in yourself or life has been disappointing to you, you can break the pattern.

You don't have to start all over, you only need to have a change of perspective.

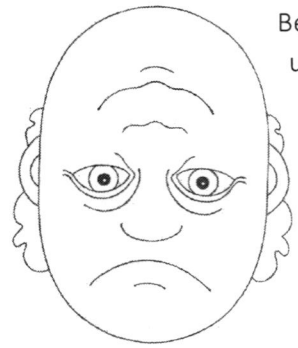

Believe you can break any of your current unproductive patterns. Figure out what you can do right now to make changes that suit you spiritually, physically, and mentally. Then, your entire being will be filled with a fresh burst of positive energy.

Take Small Steps

> *Great results come from small steps repeated every day.*

Moustafa Kadous

Rome wasn't built in a day, and you won't become the best version of yourself within a short time. If you're just getting started, start with small, easy challenges. Then, build on them. Once you've conquered the first small challenges for up to a month, consider adding new challenges to strengthen your willpower consistently.

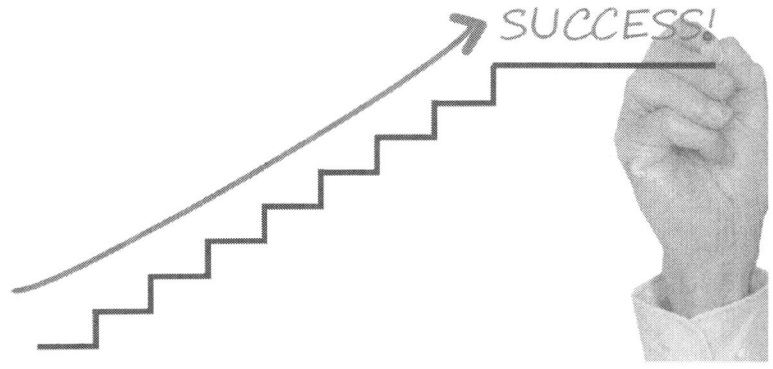

Chapter One > Actions | 27

27 | Disregard Potential Criticism and Act

> *There is only one way to avoid criticism; do nothing. Say nothing and be nothing.*
>
> *Aristotle*

Unlocking the best, you also involve resisting the temptation to remain mediocre because you want to avoid criticism. While you will encounter little or no criticism in your comfort zone, you will never have the chance to improve your current situation no matter how little.

Even if you will be criticized, the momentary pain you might experience is always greater than the pain of regret from inaction. Just do it.

It's an Experiment | 28

> *All life is an experiment; the more experiments you make the better.*

Ralph Waldo Emerson

Tell yourself, "it's an experiment" each time you want to try something new that has a very low probability of success. It will make you feel good even if you fail.

Assume the attitude that you are investing in the experiment to gather data and a return on that investment is not compulsory. The purpose of adopting this mindset is that it can lead to a permanent change if it goes well.

29 | Fall in Love with Starting, Not the Idea

> *In a startup, absolutely nothing happens unless you make it happen.*
>
> Marc Andreessen

When you share your idea with everyone, it is highly likely that you will enjoy the thrill of sharing the idea... Telling others about your plan gives you the chance to impress people with your ideas and gives you a sense of accomplishment. But you won't have done anything at all yet. What have you started?

Here's what you need to do:
- Recall and analyze your recent conversations.
- Identify a 'plan' you've always discussed but never implemented.
- Make a clear description of implementing it, and take action immediately.

Rise to the Work of a Human Being | 30

> *Don't be upset about the results you didn't get from the work you didn't do.*

Zig Ziglar

Making your life the center of laziness and comfort leads to depression in the long-term. But when you complete valuable work — which rarely feels good when you are doing something for the first time and face many challenges — the pleasure of sleeping can't match the pleasure of being productive.

Embrace discipline, and constantly improve yourself. Then, you will find fulfillment and meaning in life.

31 | Choose to Always Decide

> *If you choose not to decide, you still have made a choice.*
>
> Neil Peart

The worst decision is not to decide at all. Rather than hesitate to pursue a goal, find a low-cost way to get started. Procrastinating won't give you any additional insight. But when you go ahead and test the water, you will gain an invaluable amount of knowledge.

There Is Value in Doing Things Yourself | 32

> *Your life takes a different turn once you start doing what you truly desire.*

Moustafa Kadous

Knowledge is one reason why you should value doing things yourself. If you always pay someone else for a service, you'll never have the experience yourself. you won't truly understand what that task involves.

When you choose to do things yourself, even if it is once in a while, you will have a better understanding of others, your environment, your work, and the limit to your knowledge. These three effects give you financial and personal fulfillment when you practice this throughout your life.

Make a conscious decision about self-reliance. When next you see your well-off neighbor cutting his lawn, give him a knowing smile as you pass by because you now understand the value of doing things yourself.

33 | Work Hard... In Silence

> *Work hard in silence. Let your success be your noise.*
>
> *Frank Ocean*

While we all aspire to be successful, we need the right strategy, will power, and high aims to achieve true success in life.

Separate bad criticism from positive criticism so you can make the right corrections on your journey to success. Also, create an environment around you that's devoid of negative vibes or voices. Otherwise, you will always struggle with motivation.

Just Do It | 34

Time goes on. So, whatever you're going to do, do it. Do it now. Don't wait.

Robert De Niro

Once you notice that your procrastination is getting in the way taking action, shut off your brain because you are over-thinking it. Get hold of the basics of what you need to get started, and start immediately. These basics can be just putting on your clothes, powering on your computer, or switching off your phone.

Develop a "just do it" habit. Then, taking action becomes easier, and you won't waste valuable time going over various scenarios in your head, most of which are negative.

DO IT NOW

35 | Violent Execution

> *A good plan today is better than a perfect plan tomorrow.*

George S. Patton

While Patton's quote may seem to encourage reckless action, it's encouraging you to take action once you have a sound plan even if the plan is not perfect. If you fail to take decisive action, you will lose many opportunities.

Make your plans as best as possible, then execute immediately and with complete commitment.

Get Past Pros and Cons | 36

> *If you are trying to make a difficult decision and you're weighing the pros and cons, you have a frank decision.*

Tony Blair

Make two columns on a piece of paper. Write down all the positive outcomes in one column and all the negative ones in the second column. The winner is the column with the most entries.

However, if the entries in each column don't exactly cancel out each other, evaluate the importance of each item on the lists. Assign point values and tally them for a more realistic assessment of your options...

37 | Extreme Actions

> *We have too many high-sounding words, and too few actions that correspond with them.*
>
> *Abigail Adams*

Extreme actions – or what can also be considered extreme approaches to opportunities – entail working with great intensity for a brief period (such as a few weeks or months) to achieve certain results. After that extreme period, it's time to switch to a sustainable approach that doesn't involve as much intensity.

For example, suppose your first book becomes a best-seller. You could take the extreme approach and launch three more books in less than two months benefitting from the gained momentum. This extreme approach isn't sustainable for a long period. But it helps you to build a large following pretty quickly.

Thereafter, you can start releasing new books every year; this is a sustainable approach. The extreme approach can be likened to a sprint, while the sustainable approach can be likened to a marathon.

Purposeless Complaints | 38

Let your work speak, not your complaints.

Moustafa Kadous

Most people expend so much time and energy grumbling about everything, yet there is nothing they can do about the source of the protests. A great exercise to improve your self-control is to manage your complaints.

Starting today, go for as long as you can without complaining. Instead of complaining, find a solution. If the solution is beyond what you can proffer, let it go.

39 | Stop Blaming Society

> *...we blame the society because it's easier and a nearly impossible weight to move....*
>
> *Neil Strauss*

Using society as a crutch is easy, but you need to ask yourself whether you are only using it as an excuse not to take any action. Realize that you are not compelled to drive by your favorite fast-food joints, install a dating app, or hang out with the same people. If there is a need for you to change your surroundings, you can always move to a place that's more suitable for your personal growth.

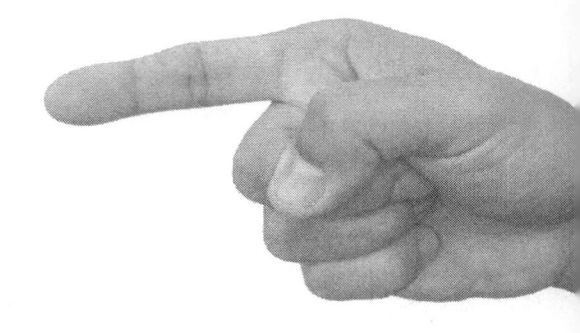

Micro-Goals | 40

> *Take a daily step that leads to your ultimate goal.*
>
> Moustafa Kadous

A micro-goal is about right now; it helps you achieve your short-term or long-term goals through small, easy, consistent, actionable steps. Try this example:
- Long-term goal: read 12 books this year
- Short-term goal: read 20 pages per day for 6 days a week
- Micro-goal: read one page right away. Then, read the next page

Turn your immediate micro-goal into a 5-minute micro-goal, and you'll be surprised at what you will accomplish. Connect micro-goals end-to-end in an upward spiral to reach your ultimate goal.

41 | Good Intentions

> It's not intentions that matter. It's actions. We are what we do and say, not what we intend to do or say.
>
> *Kristin Hannah*

While you need to identify problems, you need to solve them before you can make progress. Solving problems will involve a lot of grinding, tedious work, and making lots of difficult choices. Every good thing comes with a real price.

Dream your biggest, most magnificent dreams, but commit yourself to do all the necessary hard work to bring them into reality.

Practice It | 42

> *You make your luck, Gig. Do you know what makes a good loser? Practice.*

Ernest Hemingway

No one will accept your belief because you believe it. You need to devote your time and energy to being a living example of your belief, the simple and effective way to convince others. Put your belief into practice and combine it with strength and commitment.

43 | Practice Positively

> *A day will never be any more than what you make of it. Practice being a doer!*
>
> *Josh S. Hinds*

You become what you practice the most. Each moment has its rewards; these present moments are practices for the coming moments. When you practice love, commitment, compassion, focus, and patience, they become attracted to your life. Give your best to life and enjoy the immediate rewards and create a better future for yourself.

Choose Excellence | 44

There's no such thing as perfection. But, in striving for perfection, we can achieve excellence.

Aristotle

Doing the right thing is the way to achieve excellence, which is a display of innate honesty. Take your skills and your other resources; then move forward with excellence. Choose to spend the time and do the work you are supposed to do with excellence. You will keep enjoying the benefits of your investment in excellence many years after making the effort.

45 | Your Decision

> *Successful people make decisions based on where they want to be.*
>
> *Mel Robbins*

You don't have to allow the negative influences around you to control you. Similarly, you don't have to allow regular disappointments to discourage you. The decisions you make as you live each moment decide your ultimate end. Essentially, everything stems from your decisions.

- Decide to persist and grow stronger in the face of overwhelming obstacles. Decide to move beyond anger, bitterness, frustration, and envy into a more productive state. Decide to follow your dreams by doing whatever it takes.
- Make your decisions with careful thought and plan.

Pave Your Happiness Pathway | 46

> *Happiness is a choice, not a result. Nothing will make you happy until you choose to be happy. No person will make you happy unless you decide to be happy. Your happiness will not come to you. It can only come from you*

Ralph Marston

When you really sit down to analyze what makes you happy or will make you happy, you will realize that materialism won't create the happiness you desire. Rather, your happiness comes from living your life as authentically as you can.

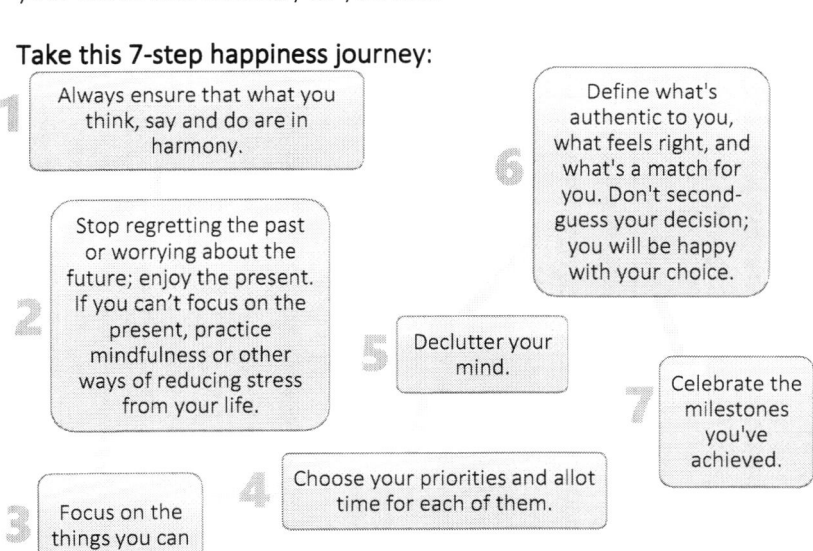

Take this 7-step happiness journey:

1. Always ensure that what you think, say and do are in harmony.

2. Stop regretting the past or worrying about the future; enjoy the present. If you can't focus on the present, practice mindfulness or other ways of reducing stress from your life.

3. Focus on the things you can control.

4. Choose your priorities and allot time for each of them.

5. Declutter your mind.

6. Define what's authentic to you, what feels right, and what's a match for you. Don't second-guess your decision; you will be happy with your choice.

7. Celebrate the milestones you've achieved.

Chapter One > Actions | 47

47 | Create Solutions Instead of Asking for Them

> *Stay away from negative people. They have a problem for every solution.*
>
> *Albert Einstein*

By relying on others' ideas and creating your own, you're resisting the temptation to be lazy. Instead of taking the easy way out, you need to seize the initiative and create solutions. Also, you need to become proactive and react as quickly as you can. Giving immediate response to situations trains you to overcome hesitation and develop action-taking habits.

Begin

Even if you don't have a perfect idea, to begin with, you can likely adapt.

Victoria Ransom

Resolve to put all the wisdom you have gained to good use. Then, begin. By now, you must have outgrown shiny distractions and flimsy excuses. So, be strong and start. The times that have passed must have made you realize you can do it. Don't hesitate again, start now to create your best future time ever.

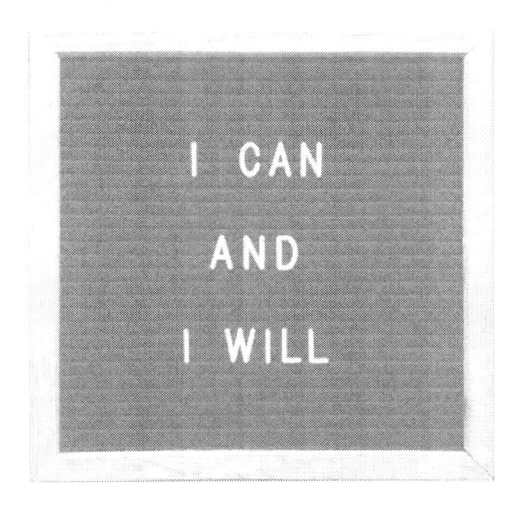

I CAN AND I WILL

49 | Decide and Act

> *One decision can change your life forever.*
>
> *Moustafa Kadous*

Decide to avoid someone, something, or some uncontrollable event to make your decision for you.

When your decision doesn't give you your desired results, you have the opportunity to adjust... Create a well-defined path to follow, and you will do great, amazing things.

Now, decide and act.

Chapter Two

OVERCOME BARRIERS & LIMITING BELIEFS

Proven tips that can help you to overcome barriers and limiting beliefs.

> Winners are not afraid of losing. But losers are. Failure is part of the process of success. People who avoid failure also avoid success.
>
> Robert Kiyosaki

50 | Overcome Your Limiting Beliefs

> *You begin to fly when you let go of self-limiting beliefs and allow your mind and aspirations to rise to greater heights.*
>
> *Brian Tracy*

You will slowly begin to see how the quality of your thoughts creates the quality of your life when you reframe your limiting beliefs into empowering ones. Once reframed, you can take small steps in changing your behavior to validate these new beliefs.

Follow this 4-step process to overcome limiting beliefs:

Step 1	Step 2	Step 3	Step 4
Recognize it.	Reject it.	Reframe it	Take one step at a time.
Examples, "I'm not..." "I can't..." "I don't have..." "it has always been this way..."		Reframe it into an empowering one. Examples, "I am..." "I can..." "I do have..." "there must be another way..."	Be willing to experience each change as it occurs. For example: "I am not a confident person" can become "I am willing to be a confident person and by taking action in areas where I lack confidence, I can prove it to myself."

Use your behavior to debunk your limiting beliefs.

52 | Chapter Two > Overcome Barriers & Limiting Beliefs

Find Fulfillment | 51

> It is not in the pursuit of happiness that we find fulfillment, it is in the happiness of pursuit.

Denis Waitley

Fulfillment comes from experiencing growth. Practicing gratitude for each growth motivates you to strive for more success and overcome your limiting beliefs.

Here are two ways I find fulfillment and recommend to you:

- Impart other people's lives. Charity works help others to feel good, and you will feel good about it as well. You don't need money to impart people, you can volunteer on a part-time basis with an NGO to help people.

- Immerse yourself in the present moment. Your anxiety and frustration will be lower while your focus, productivity, and happiness will be greater once you can connect yourself to the stillness of the here-and-now.

52 | Don't Rationalize Your Limitations with Your Age

> *We don't stop playing because we grow old; we grow old because we stop playing.*
>
> — George Bernard Shaw

While the agility of your body reduces with age, it doesn't mean you should retreat from life in itself.

Optimize what you still have and surround yourself with mentally young people. Then, you won't become one of those bitter old people who has passed away mentally and is only living to experience physical death.

Overcome Your Invisible Prison Bars

> *There are plenty of difficult obstacles in your path. Don't allow yourself to become one of them.*

Ralph Marston

A wrong choice is taking the path of most resistance when working on your strengths or weaknesses. A better option is to focus on improving your strengths to the extent that it comes to you naturally. Then, you can maximize the benefits that unlock the best in you.

54 | Increase Your Eustress

> *When life gives you stress, make it eustress, not distress.*
>
> *Siddhartha Puri*

Eustress (the opposite of distress) helps you to respond to stress with healthy, positive feelings.

Positive forms of social engagement, communal support, and resourcefulness can trigger eustress. Any strenuous activity that creates feelings of pleasure or joy is eustress.

If the same activity creates feelings of anxiety, depression, or worry, then it is distress. Positive self-talk and re-affirming statements to yourself can be very powerful and can eliminate negative perceptions of most stress responses.

Let's consider winning the lottery as a sudden event that promotes change in all areas of the winner. Then, it is a stressor.

Suppose persons A and B are two winners of the lottery. If after winning the lottery,

- Person A starts to worry about being kidnapped or robbed. This person is experiencing negative stress. This negative stress is distress.
- Person B starts creating projects to bring his dreams to reality. This person is experiencing positive stress, or eustress.

Make eustress a part of your daily life:
- Engage in regular physical exercise.
- Learn a new skill or taking on a new responsibility.
- Learn how to set challenging but realistic goals. Don't forget to hold yourself accountable by tracking your progress.

55 | Pay the Price Fast

> *There is always a way to get out no matter how long a situation continues. But the sooner you handle it, the easier it is.*

Harry Browne

When you allow small irritating things to continue, they grow into bigger problems. So, you need to develop the habit of resolving unpleasant situations immediately to prevent them from getting worse and becoming more difficult to handle. A side benefit of doing this is that it boosts your willpower muscle.

Harness Positive Attitudes | 56

> *Life is 10% what happens to you and 90% how you react to it.*

Charles R. Swindoll

Those who become the best in life and business are those who have a positive outlook and believe that they can attain it. There is more to positive thinking than improving your attitude; it involves expanding your capacity for success (regardless of your definition of success). Your thoughts and words about your desires make you feel happy and in full control of your life. When you have happy thoughts, your brain releases endorphins which makes you feel good. As a result, you have a positive attitude.

You'll need a network of support to make a positive change in your life. Start by asking your loved ones to make you realize it when you show a negative change in your attitude.

Tell them, "I am trying to change my perspective of life by eliminating negative thinking. So, when you hear me speak negatively, let me know. I'll appreciate it a lot."

57 | Go On "Vice Fasts"

> *Be always at war with your vices, at peace with your neighbors and let each new year find you a better man.*

Benjamin Franklin

Then, feast on the virtues. If you're multitasking to keep a healthy level of motivation, cut yourself some slack, and tackle one habit at a time. If you're channeling your willpower into places you don't desire, re-evaluate your decisions to sift out the most important ones. Finally, if you want to achieve healthy behaviors, seek out groups with similar goals as yours.

Take Each Process as a Litmus Test | 58

> *The shortest way to do many things is to do one at a time.*

Samuel Smiles

How you imagine the process of achieving your goal is a litmus test that determines whether or not you are pursuing the right goals in the right manner. If you have a plan to achieve your goal, but the plan is completely uninspiring – hard and broken down into countless frustrating steps – add fun to each step you complete.

For example, you can give yourself regular rewards, anything that makes you feel good. Spend a few minutes playing a fun online game, or take a walk along a nature path.

59 | Avoid Dangerous Venues

> *Avoid what causes the opposite of what you want to achieve.*
>
> *Peter Bevelin*

Want to become more productive? Do away with what lazy people consider as must-haves. Want to stop drinking alcohol? Stop attending parties where alcohol is the main source of entertainment. The point is, figure out the opposite of your goals.

Then, find out places, people, and actions that can lead to such opposites and avoid them.

Reduce the Procrastination from Overwhelm | 60

> *You have a greater tendency to procrastinate when the project seems bigger and more overwhelming.*

Neil Fiore

When some people consider the importance of learning something, it overwhelms them, paralyzes their actions, and leads to procrastination. You are likely to be more self-conscious (and possibly, procrastinate) when you assume something is your only big chance in life.

When setting new resolutions, avoid overwhelm by managing your attitude about them; keep a cool head about them. Don't let the overwhelm lead to procrastination.

61 | The All-or-Nothing Mentality Can Be Derailing

> *One setback is one setback - it is not the end of the world, and it's not the end of your journey towards a better you.*
>
> *Jillian Micheals*

Those who can't see how they can make it big right away don't act on their goals. For such people, it's either it occurs completely or it doesn't occur at all.

If small slip-ups discourage you from making further efforts, remind yourself that you are allowed to stick with 90% of your resolutions while the 10% leftover is your margin for error. Since you've already accounted for it, it won't destroy your entire progress.

When You Think You Are Not Good Enough | 62

> *We can't hate ourselves into a version of ourselves we can love.*

Lori Deschene

It's easy to feel like we're falling behind or not just good enough when we see other people's success on social media. Recognizing that "good enough" or "bad enough" comes from within is the best way to deal with it. You must train your mind to stop engaging in negative thoughts.

When a negative thought comes up, imagine placing the thought on a little boat and allowing it to float away on water. Then, you don't have to stop those negative thoughts, which can be a struggle; you can train your mind to let go of the negative thoughts. However, you need to practice this regularly until it becomes natural.

63 | "If Only I Had More Money"

> *If only...the saddest words in the English language.*
>
> Kristan Higgins

That quote can sabotage a thorough self-examination and prevent you from making decisions that can lead to the enjoyment of the present. It is easy to say that a lack of excuse is your ultimate excuse for not going after your goals. But is it true? Are you saying you can't save one dollar a day to establish a new positive habit? Are all your purchases necessary? Or, can't you reduce them even by a small fraction?

Seek a solution instead of using money as an excuse; you will benefit from future improvements in your life.

A Cleaner Immediate Environment Creates Better Feelings | 64

> *People exert more self-control after seeing a clean desk than after seeing a messy desk.*

Roy Baumeister

The distractions from a chaotic surrounding environment lowers productivity and affects your self-esteem. Think about it, you feel better when you perform your grooming habits; put on make-up, shave your face, and take a shower.

The way dressing for success boosts your confidence is the same way keeping a neat and tidy environment boosts your productivity levels.

65 | Eliminate Excuses

> *If you want to do something, you'll find a way. If you don't, you'll find an excuse.*
>
> *Jim Rohn*

Strangely, we usually start giving excuses when something is important to us. A way to not find excuses instead of having to eliminate it is to trust yourself to think of a solution when excuse situations arise. Also, list every worst-case scenario and think of ways to eliminate all of them. You might even recognize a theme that makes it easy to tackle the excuse in one swoop.

Exceed Your Limits | 66

> *There are no limitations to the mind except those we acknowledge.*

Napoleon Hill

If there is a limit, it means you can't go beyond that boundary or barrier. But the question is, who defines your limits? Since you define your limits, you can change them.

There are two main steps to exceeding your limits. The first step is to be aware of the limits you have defined for yourself which now forms part of your belief. Then, the second step is to identify facts that prove you can do what seems impossible for you.

I recommend that you enlist the help of a friend or coach; you will gain a different perspective of the same belief.

67 | Look Fear in the Face

> The cave you fear to enter holds the treasure you seek.
>
> *Joseph Campbell*

When you are afraid, look fear in the face and send it packing. Then, when next it appears, you'll be confident to say, "I overcame it once; I will overcome it again." With regular practice, you'll become less susceptible to temptations and even more likely to ignore those fears.

Change Your Mind; Be Flexible | 68

> *You might need to constantly readjust to your surroundings so that you can apply the new knowledge you've acquired.*

Moustafa Kadous

As long as you apply it in the right circumstances, self-discipline remains a powerful force. However, when your efforts are fruitless and unlikely to yield any positive results, exerting self-control blindly is a waste of time and can lead to bitterness.

Revise your methods periodically based on any new information you have acquired. Ask yourself, "Is there a need to make changes and refocus your efforts? If yes, make those changes.

69 | Identify Your Resources

> *Do what you can with all you have wherever you are.*
>
> — *Theodore Roosevelt*

You have a resource or an ability you can tap to overcome every problem you face. The key is to discover that resource and put it to good use. Instead of adopting a resourceful attitude and looking for solutions, most people default to frustration or discouragement.

A simple and effective way to prepare for setbacks is to visualize them. Next, while you're still on top of your game without the influence of negative emotions, create a list of potential solutions. Then, when you have a clouded mind, you will use this list for possible solutions which also saves you time and energy.

Success and Positivity | 70

> *Your positive action combined with positive thinking results in success.*

Shiv Khera

Though life produces great challenges constantly, it also provides meaning and fulfillment to those that prepare for the challenges and overcome them.

If you're not satisfied with your current realities, use it as an opportunity to make a difference, and be the difference. Don't take it as an excuse to be dejected.

Having a strong, non-negotiable positive vision is the way to get past obstacles. Let your best vision drive you to be among the unique, creative, and resourceful people working their way to make life better. It is highly likely that you will be a success.

71 | Get Past Tough Situations Quickly

> *Rough times never last, tough people do.*
>
> Robert Schuller

One day almost everything is going according to plan. Then, the unexpected happens. You lose your home, a loved one, your job, or even your health. Even though you don't deserve it or plan for it, you need to deal with it and move on with your life.

Here are tips you'll find helpful:

- Stop going on an unfair spiral. Remind yourself of the realities on the ground. Then, reaction the way you'd like your world to be.
- Remind yourself that a hurdle can't obliterate your plans. If you lose your job, pursue other professional goals with greater efficiency. You can address a problem in more than one way.

Become a Master Problem-Solver | 72

Solve a real problem and the world is yours.

Aaron Patzer

Hone this skill to save time, make money, and find the next big idea for your business.

- Ask lots of questions to identify the correct problem.
- Brainstorm all possible solutions, including bouncing ideas off others.
- Evaluate the ideas above based on the complexity of each idea and their impact on the goal.
- Create a plan to execute the idea.
- Track the solution's progress to be sure you're still on the right track.

73 | Explore New Opportunities

> *You never change your life until you step out of your comfort zone; change begins at the end of your comfort zone.*

Roy T. Bennett

It is safe and predictable to do the same thing every day, but it can result in inaction and a habit to resist change. Push yourself into unfamiliar places and do things you wouldn't do normally.

Look at all the inventions in the world today. None of them would have been accomplished without people who stepped out of their comfort zones.

If there is an opportunity you can explore, find ways you can figure it out, and make it happen.

Explore Your Creative Side | 74

Creativity is intelligence having fun.

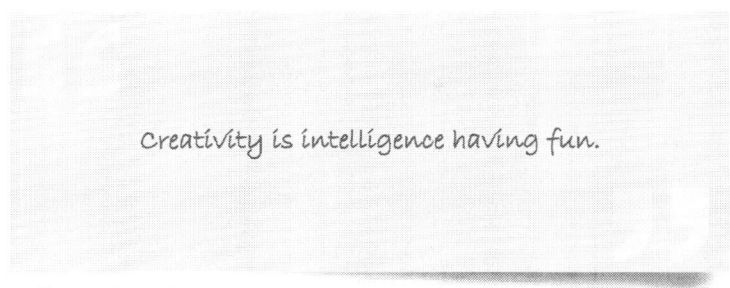

Albert Einstein

Most of us are yet to tap or maximize the fountain of creativity within us. Regardless of the form, creativity helps us to utilize parts of our mind yet to be tapped, have a different perspective on problems and solutions, then grow professionally and personally.

Explore your creative side by trying new things:

- Join a music group, learn a new instrument, or play an instrument.
- Try landscape photography, bird watching or gardening.
- Make pottery, sculpt or paint.
- Perform any activity you've never explored fully, haven't practiced in years or you have never tried.

75 | Expand Your Mind

> *What you focus on expands...*
>
> *Esther Jno-Charles*

When you nurture your mind and body, you have more physical and mental endurance, greater strength, more ideas, compassion, knowledge, and energy.

Grow and maintain your mental ability by keeping your mind active.

- Read anything and everything.
- Join an organization or group with people from diverse cultures, attend performances and listen to different music styles.
- Use your brain to perform simple calculations instead of using a calculator.
- Play board games that involve strategy.

Don't Let Anyone Tell You Your Potential | 76

> *Amaze yourself, manifest your full potential.*

Mark Victor Hansen

Visualize yourself for who you are, who you desire to be, and who you will eventually be. Then, you will have strength for your present and your future.

Believing what other people say about your limits will prevent you from achieving success even if you are capable of going beyond such limits.

Define your true potential and you will discover that you are limitless.

77 | Avoid Self-Sabotage

> *Don't be the obstacle to your progress.*
>
> *Moustafa Kadous*

Becoming aware of self-sabotaging behaviors is the first step to breaking its cycle. Perfectionism is a common self-sabotaging behavior. Identifying self-sabotage behaviors helps you focus on specific changes you need to make to stop these behaviors.

Perform self-reflection to gain vital understanding, perspective, and insights. Then, you can start the process of change and transformation.

Life Is a Climb | 78

Enthusiasm is the great hill-climber

Elbert Hubbard

Imagine your goal is a steep hill, and you're scrambling up slowly. Do you think you can stop midway? Absolutely not. That's what most people do when the path to their goal seems longer than expected. At the same time, a slow start doesn't mean it will remain that way till the end.

You should aim to reach the goal even if it takes longer than planned. As long as you are moving towards your goal, don't stop. Keep moving because your speed doesn't matter, moving forward does.

79 | Above Thoughtlessness

> *Be daring. Be first. Be different.*
>
> Anita Roddick

It is an open secret; no one will treat you the way you want to be treated all the time. So, resolve to accept that fact. By rising above the thoughtless, negative behavior of others, you can exercise and expand your strength.

Always keep in mind that most people deal with their fears and insecurities by being rude or hurtful.

Be the model of how a positive, accepting attitude can result in a more positive world.

Break the Cycle | 80

The only option I have is to step up and pave my pathway.

Moustafa Kadous

Have you failed to live up to your intentions, expectations, or standards? Change direction now.

If you keep wallowing in that disappointment in yourself, it will set you up for more disappointment.

Make decisions and choices that can turn that restrictive feeling of disappointment into inspiring energy of action and fulfillment.

81 | The Source of Fulfillment

> *Be careful what you set your heart upon;*
> *for it will surely be yours.*
>
> *James Baldwin*

There are values and joy in each action and each step through life. Enjoy it. Regardless of the task, love and appreciate the present moments, and you'll find joy doing the task.

When you make negative assumptions, your work becomes harder. For example, when you assume a task will be tedious, then it will be truly difficult.

Find the joy in each step of your journey, and you'll experience fulfillment well before you complete the journey.

One at a Time | 82

> It's better to do one thing well than ten things poorly.

Heather Hart

You'll end up with frustration trying to make everything better at once. But you can make it better little by little, and it will compound greatly over time. If you want to shed ten pounds, you can't lose everything by next week. You can lose a pound next week and each week thereafter until you lose all ten pounds.

Use the time you have to do what you can and when you can. By starting now, you can take control of your destiny and keep going.

Chapter Three

INSPIRATION & MOTIVATION

Steps that inspire and motivate you to take action.

> Motivation gets you going, and habits gets you there. Make motivation your guide, and you will get there more quickly and have more fun on the trip.
> — Zig Ziglar

83 | Give Genuine Compliments

> *Too often, we underestimate the power of a touch, a smile, a kind word, a listening ear, an honest compliment or the smallest act of caring, all of which have the potential to turn a life around.*
>
> *Leo Buscaglia*

Empathy is a vital part of showing genuine compliments. Looking for the good of others is a big step towards bringing out the best in you in a world filled with cynicism and negativity.

Tell someone what you genuinely think is special about them instead of telling him what you think he wants to hear.

However, you must be honest when giving your true compliments; put yourself in the person's shoes.

Be Motivated to Get Up Early | 84

> You've got to get up every morning with determination if you're going to go to bed with satisfaction.

George Horace Lorimer

Set an exciting expectation for each coming day. A good expectation might be a long-term goal that requires your daily input. It will keep you from staying in bed for more than necessary. Having a good reason to wake up is more helpful than any "wake up" tricks, such as putting your alarm across the room or tracking your sleep phases.

Plan to perform an activity you love during your early mornings. If your goal is exciting, you'll always associate early rising with something pleasant. Then, you have the motivation to get out of bed once the alarm goes off. Also, create a morning mantra. For example, "I choose to wake up today because I need to [include a personal benefit here]." Write it and stick it in an obvious place where you'll see it immediately when you wake up. For optimal results, you can write a new mantra for each day.

85 | Seek Inspiration and Act

> *Genius is 1% inspiration and 99% perspiration.*
>
> *Thomas Edison*

While inspiration can come from times and places you least expect, successful people know that success requires action. So, don't talk about what you need to do, just get out there and start doing it now.

Here are ways to turn your inspiration into action:

- Take notes. When you read a book or listen to an audio, create a summary of what you've just learned. For optimal results, you can doodle on it with your pen.
- Stop spending hours reading a list of inspiring quotes. Reflect upon what it means, decide how you can apply the inspiration in your life, and act upon it.
- Learn on the go, especially when getting started with a new venture. Resist the urge to know everything before you start; just know the first step, act on it, and learn along the way.

Be Open to Feedback | 86

> *If any man can convince me and prove to me that I don't think or act right, I will gladly change....*

Marcus Aurelius

If you keep going on the wrong path stubbornly, it can result in a lot of wasted time. Be open to feedback from those who've accomplished the goals you want to achieve, especially when you have no real-world experience about the goal. It will save you from unnecessary failures.

87 | Regularized Motivation

> *...motivation is not permanent. But then, neither is bathing; but it is something you should do regularly.*
>
> *Zig Ziglar*

Never assume you will be motivated forever because you're motivated now. Also, never give up on your goals because you lack motivation temporarily. You need to replenish your motivation whenever it drops, and sometimes, you may have to find new motivators.

Document what fires you up. For example, inspirational articles, inspirational images, and motivational songs. When you lack motivation, lift your spirits by accessing this "inspiration bank."

Prosocial Motivation | 88

> *"Be the person that makes other people feel important."*

Moustafa Kadous

If not for your benefit, considering the benefits of your actions with others can shake you out of inaction. Take time to consider the negative impact of your inaction on your loved ones and friends.

Some people derive more motivation from this exercise than any motivational words or speech.

If you care about others more than yourself, this motivation can turn you into a high achiever.

89 | Self-Goals and Self-Control

> *"People with goals succeed because they know where they're going."*
>
> *Earl Nightingale*

Link your goals with its intrinsic benefits. For example, what is the link between building a business and your need for learning or autonomy? A business lets you control your life to the fullest and give you financial freedom.

Go through the same thought process with your goals. The goals' importance increases within you and makes you more determined to achieve them.

Choose a Specific Cue and a Clear Reward | 90

> *People who have successfully started new exercise routines prove that they can stick with a workout plan provided they have the right cue and the right reward.*

Charles Duhigg

A habit is a combination of a cue and a reward that creates an automatic behavior when both the cue and reward loop are performed repeatedly.

If you want to create new routines with less resistance, ensure that you have clear cues and rewards. However, make sure your reward doesn't undo the benefits of the habit. For instance, instead of eating a giant pizza as a reward for exercising, a healthier, less-caloric reward — such as a smoothie, some nuts, or a piece of fruit — will be a better option.

91 | Find Fun in the Impossible

> *Impossible means only means haven't found the solution yet.*
>
> *Henry Ford*

If you're starting from zero, becoming a millionaire in five years isn't impossible; becoming a billionaire might be unlikely. A way to test the concept of impossible goals that push your resolve is to set a goal with a short deadline. For example, master a foreign language in three months. If you treat this fun experiment seriously, you might be surprised at your accomplishment.

Give Yourself Self-Compassion | 92

> *Allow yourself to be a beginner. No one starts off being excellent.*

Wendy Flynn

Each time you are unable to meet your standards, remind yourself that you put in your best efforts, only that they were not enough. Rather than mope about your failure, you'll be better off learning from the slip-up and avoiding the repetition of the same mistakes next time.

All the self-criticism in this world won't do you any good. Your motivation to try again will come from being kind to yourself.

93 | Inspire Yourself to Give Up Negative Behaviors

> *Find your voice and inspire others to find theirs.*
>
> *Stephen Covey*

How well you tolerate problems in your life determines how you limit your possibilities. If you perceive that the negative consequences of your harmful actions or bad habits are weak, it is highly likely that you will keep tolerating them as long it doesn't increase.

A good way to inspire yourself to give up negative behaviors is to make yourself aware of the pain's depth. Tune into it and focus on all its consequences; assume that the pain will get worse. Inspire the change with negative visualization.

Change Your Identity When It Doesn't Work for You | 94

> *Identity cannot be found or fabricated but emerges from within when one dares to let go.*

Doug Cooper

Changing your identity is the only way to enforce a permanent change. Your efforts to change will be in vain as long as you define yourself by the behavior you want to eliminate. Subconsciously, you will be treating your changes as a temporary situation.

Accept the present but create a unique, positive definition of yourself that explains your personality and your current realities, not your past personality or old realities.

95 | Valuable Feedback from Failure

> *You will learn more from your failures than your successes.*
>
> *Moustafa Kadous*

For most people, failure is caused by an external factor, sometimes just luck. As a result, they fail to identify opportunities from these failures.

Each time you fail, look for the cause of the failure from things you can control or things you did and not from what's outside your control. Then, you won't repeat the same mistakes in your future attempts. Also, you will develop the mindset that you have direct influence over your life.

Quit Smartly | 96

> *The best quitters are those who decide in advance when they will quit....*

Seth Godin

Sometimes, it is more beneficial to quit than stubbornly stick with something that's not working for you. The secret is to quit smartly, and you can only quit smartly when you engage in logical thinking instead of taking impulsive decisions.

If you're discouraged with the path to one of your goals, don't quit till you've made a logical, educated decision that considers all the consequences of your decision.

97 | Find the Weak Points in Your Armor

> *Two things define you: your patience when you have nothing and your attitude when you have everything.*

Imam Ali

The weakest point in your armor is the one that poses the biggest barrier to achieving your goals or tempts you the most. Impatience with the process that leads to the goal is an example of a weak point.

Examine the impact of your weak points on your goals and seek long-lasting solutions.

Draw Inspiration from the Greats | 100

> Inspiration exists, but it has to find you working.

Pablo Picasso

Somebody, somewhere in the past has faced the problems you are facing today. These problems may not be exactly as yours, but close enough such that you can relate with the person's story. It is for this reason that I recommend reading autobiographies and biographies. You can apply their lessons to your life and rest assured their lessons could work for you as it worked for them.

101 | Constructive Non-Conformity

> *Always think outside the box and embrace opportunities that appear, wherever they might be.*

Elon Musk

Asking "why," "how might we...?" and "what...?" place conflicting issues side-by-side so you can start solving for them as a team. You can only come up with new thinking by challenging "the way you do it today." For example, ask your people to imagine that they work for your competitor, and they have been assigned to attack your organization at its weakest point. Through this activity, you can identify new issues from another point of view.

Seek Knowledge, Not Results | 102

> *Chase the vision, not the money. The money will end up following you.*

Tony Hsieh

If the results are your focus, your motivation will always fluctuate, and it'll die the moment you hit a storm. Keep your motivation fueled by focusing on the excitement of discovery, experimenting, exploring, and improving. Think of the lessons being learned and what you need to improve; the results will follow.

103 | Find Strength in Unity

> *Alone we can do so little; together we can do so much.*

Helen Keller

Understand that you don't have to go at it alone to develop unmatched mental toughness. Build a team of supporters that will step in and back you up during important moments. One such support is a good mentor or group of mentors. A good coach will help you work through your weaknesses, overcome your blind spots, and discover your greatest strengths.

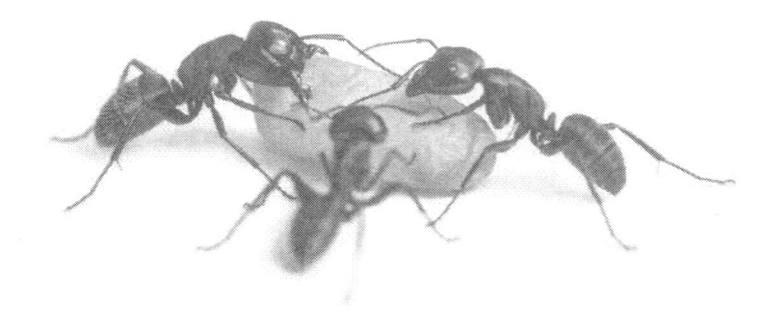

Pick Yourself Back Up After Setbacks | 104

> *Don't allow a setback or two to give you an excuse to sit back. Pick yourself up and continue to move forward.*

Dr. K. L. Register

Instead of giving up when you find yourself in a low spot, ask yourself these questions that help you re-evaluate your current mindset:

- Do I still need to accomplish this goal? If yes, why?
- What's my true purpose for achieving my goal?
- What are the lessons from these setbacks?
- Are my thoughts an obstruction to my focus or view?
- Am I overworking myself or aiming too high, which puts me under unnecessary pressure?

105 | The Wonder

> *There are many wonderful things that will never be done if you do not do them....*
>
> *Charles D. Gill*

Imagine a life without anxiety, worry, fear, or pain. A life where it's only you and the wonder of the existence surrounding you.

Ever since time began, this unique, magical wonder has existed. You only need to create space for its energy to fill your spirit and encourage you to move forward with inspired purpose.

Imagine this wonder and live what you imagine.

Get Better | 106

When you improve yourself, things get easier.

Moustafa Kadous

There is a good chance that things are about to get better when it seems that they are getting worse.

The opportunities for positive progress grow bigger in the same way as challenges. Become highly motivated to make things right when everything seems to be going wrong.

Take bold, positive, and focused action when times are tough.

107 | Uncover Lessons from Your Illness

> *Circumstances do not make the man; they merely reveal him to himself.*
>
> *Epictetus*

During or after recovering from an illness, you can learn a lot about how to be happy and what it truly means to live a good life. Instead of constantly pushing yourself to be more and more productive, you can create a schedule for rest and focus on the healthy habits you'll need to feel better. Don't feel guilty or lazy when you have to rest; it's medicine.

Chapter Four

INNER STRENGTH & CONFIDENCE

Actionable tips on how to channel your innate power to boost your confidence and achieve your goals.

> "The only thing standing between you and your goal is the bullshit story you keep telling yourself as to why you can't achieve it."
>
> — Jordan Belfort

108 | Discover Your Inner Beauty

> *You have to rely on whatever sparks you have inside.*
>
> *Lisa Kleypas*

Your confidence, which grows from your inner strength, can greatly affect another person's perception of you. Your greatest successes will come from using your inner power to maximize the good times. Then, when times are rough, your strong inner core will get you through.

No one is perfect and there are things you can improve about yourself. But you should strive to improve them based on your decision and not the opinion of others. Make small daily changes that add up to the new you that you desire. Being proud of your current character is the key to using your inner strength to improve your outer beauty.

Maximize the Present Moments | 109

> *The present moment consists of the past and the future. The secret of transformation is how we handle the present moment.*

Thich Nhat Hanh

With each present moment, you are given a blank check to improve your life, and it starts with making one decision. As you go about your day, realize that each of your little choices affects your future. Then, reinforce positive habits so that you can re-engage in it in the future.

Personal transformation happens in the present; it doesn't happen in the future. Make decisions that ensure your transformation is in the right direction.

110 | Deepen Your Intuition

> *You can't access your intuition without connecting with it.*

Moustafa Kadous

You need to deepen your connection to your intuition before you can access it. Meditation is the best tool for deepening your connection.

With regular meditation, your mind is free from distractions and you can recognize subtle cues within you. Ten minutes of meditation per day is enough to achieve incredible results.

Strengthen Your Willpower | 111

> *Many men and women in the world demonstrate great willpower and self-discipline in overcoming bad habits and the weaknesses of the flesh.*

Ezra Taft Benson

With the right practice, you can strengthen your willpower. Training your willpower is similar to training for a marathon. You might not complete the full 26 miles on your first training. But with time, your muscles become stronger, and you can complete the full distance.

Similarly, tracking the food you eat can help you avoid poor snacking. Also, creating self-imposed deadlines can help you to tune out distractions, become hyper-productive, and improve your willpower.

You might struggle with it in the short-term. But over time, you will have the willpower to reject temptations, and stick to your long-term goals.

112 | Choose Your Response to Pain

> *Pain is a strategy. If you know how to use it.*
>
> Tony Robbins

Want to put yourself in uncomfortable situations for the sake of bigger and better future rewards? Separate yourself from temporary pain. Sometimes, pain is inevitable in most actions that require effort. Your response to your pain will either hinder your progress or further it.

Each time you feel temporary pain or discomfort – not the kind that can cause an accident or the sign of an impending injury, but emotional or minor physical discomfort – refuse to associate with it mentally. Make the pain fade into the background, and move past it.

"This, Too, Shall Pass" | 113

> *Life is short, but it is wide. This, too, shall pass.*

Rebecca Wells

Everything in this world is ephemeral and transient: the good, the bad, pleasures, torments, boredom, and even excitement. While the pleasures and excitement provide you with optimism that there is light at the end of your dark tunnel, it also reminds you to cherish the good things you currently have because those, too, shall pass.

114 | Know That You Have the Power to Change

> *You have the power to change your thoughts, and your thoughts have the power to change your life.*

Ron Willingham

Though it is unsatisfying and miserable, why do you still stay in a job, relationship, or location you hate? Always keep in mind that you are the only one who can control how and where you spend your time, including any benefits you will derive from it. You are the pilot, the director, the person in charge, and you have the power to change direction when you need it.

One proven way to use this power is to strengthen your self-esteem. Journal the times when your self-confidence led to your success, and imagine yourself repeating the same thing during your current predicament.

Replace Can'ts with Don'ts | 115

> *I don't' is experienced as a choice; it's an affirmation of your determination and willpower. 'I can't' is a restriction imposed on you. An 'I can't' perspective undermines your sense of power and personal agency.*

Heidi Grant Halverson

When you have to give up something to make a new, positive change in your life, never say "I can't." By using the words "I can't," you are viewing your decision from a perspective of restriction. Another way to give up something is to tie it with the negative consequences that you don't want to experience.

Replace "I can" with "I don't;" it leads to a choice that makes you want to prevent the unpleasant consequences. This small change in vocabulary can result in a temporary or permanent impact on the changes you're trying to accomplish.

116 | Allow Confidence to Take Over

> *If a voice within you says, 'you cannot do something,' then most certainly start doing that thing, and you will silence that voice.*
>
> *Moustafa Kadous*

If you have been living in doubt and fear for too long, it is time to adopt an attitude of confidence. You can surmount any challenge and enjoy the success that comes with it.

Get yourself into the mindset that you are not only capable of doing it, but you can be the best at it.

Arouse the confidence that has been within you all this time, and let it push any remaining doubt or indecision that's left behind. Then, bring to life your full creative potential.

Manage Your Energy | 117

> *Your energy is your currency; spend it wisely.*

Bianca Bass

By establishing specific rituals, intentionally practiced behaviors and precisely scheduled behaviors, you can systematically expand your and feel renewed. Regardless of the circumstances you're facing, recognize the costs of energy-depleting behaviors and take responsibility for changing them.

Find out the time of the day when you are at peak energy levels. Then, honor these energy levels. Use the 'trough' periods to take a 10- or 20-minute power nap, do stretches, or take a quick walk.

118 | Don't Undermine Your Self-Trust

> *Self-trust is the first secret of success.*
>
> *Ralph Waldo Emerson*

I value the agreements I make with myself in the same way I value the agreements I make with other people. The way you lose the trust of others when you don't keep your promise is the same way you lose the trust of yourself when you fail to keep an agreement you made with yourself.

Honor the commitments you make with yourself just like you honor the ones you make with others.

Value Other People's Insights | 119

> *Be humble, be hungry, and always be the hardest worker in the room.*

Dwayne Johnson

Don't build relationships with people that will stroke your ego. You'll be isolating yourself from reality and surrounding yourself with "yes people," which is just like talking to yourself.

Stay grounded; never stop growing. Value other people's opinions and insights. Don't open your mouth until you have listened to other peoples' opinions.

120 | Amplify Your Confidence

> *As is our confidence, so is our capacity.*

William Hazlitt

As humans, two voices reside within us. One nurtures and uplifts, which inspires confidence. The other criticizes and discourages, our inner critic. Once you learn how to give less power to the voice of the inner critic, you will give more fuel to the voice that amplifies your confidence.

These top habits can fuel the voice that amplifies your confidence:
- Mindful meditation. You will start experiencing a change in the way you think once you realize that you are not your thoughts; you are just an observer of your thoughts. Positive thoughts about yourself create positive feelings about yourself.
- Practice self-compassion. Be kind to yourself during times of emotional distress or perceived failure.
- Believe in your abilities. Self-belief will spark your confidence and you can dive into new experiences that are far beyond your comfort zones.

Join Like Minds | 121

> *Be friends with people who want the same wants as you.*
>
> Moustafa Kadous

Peer pressure can be a beneficial tool for an adult who joins a group whose attributes he'd like to acquire. So, join a group of people with whom you have a common objective and let their influence change you for good.

Want to exercise regularly? Join a fitness group. Want to stop impulse expenses? Join a personal finance forum. Don't join groups who don't exhibit the traits you'd like to acquire.

122 | Create Your Fashion Style

> *Fashion is what you buy, style is what you do with it.*
>
> — *Nicky Hilton*

Being trendy and fashionable impacts your self-confidence and other people's perception of you.

Your clothing reminds you of the need to make healthy choices. While your wardrobe can grow with you, your style can remain the same at its core since it's an extension of you. Choose any style that makes you comfortable and confident.

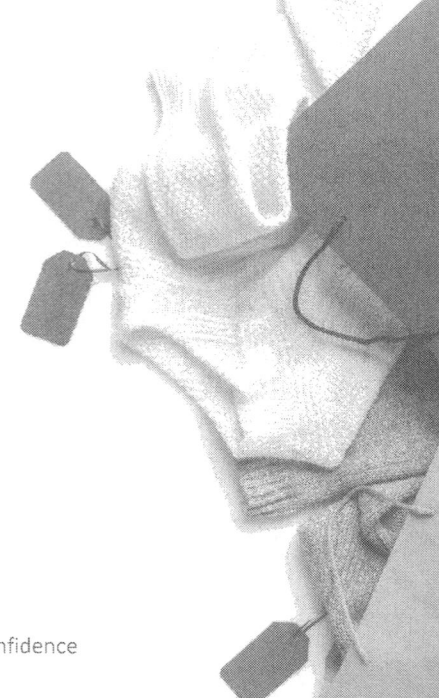

Dominate Every First Impression | 123

> *Almost everyone will make a good first impression, but only a few will make a good lasting first impression.*

Sonya Parker

Just as a picture speaks a thousand words, so does the first impression speak a thousand words.

Each time you meet a new person, regardless of the location, smile, and be mindful of your body language. You will leave the person with a great and lasting first impression while your self-confidence will improve as well.

124 | Unlearn Your Need to be Liked by Everyone

> *You are not chocolate; you can't make everyone happy.*
>
> *Moustafa Kadous*

Have these thoughts ever crossed your mind:

"Would people like what I do, say, or create?"
"What would people say about my looks?"

We've all harbored these thoughts at one point or another because it is a fundamental human need to want to be liked. However, these thoughts can stop you from finding your true self.

Resisting your people-pleasing reflex is about going after things your way and for you. It's not about chasing someone else's approval, writing off responsibilities, or being rude. What you need to do is to stop tying your worth to the likes." Always remind yourself that your worth doesn't require anyone else's approval.

Juggle the Five Balls | 125

> *Suppose life is a game where you have to juggle five balls in the air. The balls are work, family, health, friends, and integrity. There will come a day you will realize that you can drop the work ball, and it will bounce back because it is a rubber ball. But the other balls will shatter completely without repair because they are made of glass.*

James Patterson

Always prioritize glass balls over the rubber ones as you balance different aspects of your life. While you can always accomplish your goals later, you can't always regain trust, recover your health, revive your friendships, or restore your relationship with your family.

Spend five minutes today to perform a thorough analysis of how you are handling the glass balls in your life. For instance, are you focusing on your work and ignoring your health?

126 | Two Alternatives

> *Happiness is a conscious choice, not an automatic response.*
>
> Mildred Barthel

You have two alternatives when things go wrong. You can make those things better or worse. You can use the situation as an inspiration or use it to feel sorry for yourself. Don't add to the disappointments through your actions or bad choices.

Regardless of the unfairness, unjustness, or disappointment of life and in life, decide to look ahead, act ahead, and live ahead so that you can get ahead.

You Always Have More Than Two Options | 127

Right now, your range of available choices is unlimited.

Frederick Carl Frieseke

One way to sabotage yourself is to assume that you only have two options. When you think that way, you lose your power of choice. It's highly likely that you won't make any decision if you're not satisfied with the available options. The truth is there are always more than two options.

Black or white thinking is mental laziness. The next time you think that you are limited to two options have a proper re-think; more options are available to you. Give yourself a better chance of making the right decision by searching for at least one more option.

Chapter Five

FORGIVENESS, LETTING GO & BALANCE

Tips to forgive and let go, achieve work-life balance, take care of your body, and enjoy peace of mind.

> "Emotions are what makes us human. Make us real. The word "emotion" stands for energy in motion. Be truthful about your emotions, and use your mind and emotions in your favor, not against yourself."
>
> — Robert Kiyosaki

128 | Give Up Having the Last Word

> *Have the maturity to know that sometimes silence is more powerful than having the last word.*
>
> *Thema Davis*

When you think about it deeply, your reason for wanting to have the last word is to make the other person feel worse. Instead of making the person feel worse, why not agree to disagree by changing the topic of discussion to a more pleasant one.

When you learn how to exercise self-restraint, you will not only improve your relationships with others, you will also improve your self-control.

Let Go, Stay Focused, and Move Forward | 129

> *When I let go of what I am, I become what I might be.*

Lao Tzu

Most of us don't know how to let go of the past. Sadly, holding on to the past is a form of self-sabotage because it won't give you the freedom to look beyond.

Follow these four steps to letting go:

- Acknowledge the pain and be willing to see it through.
- Focus only on what you can learn from the past.
- Create a positive narrative and positive emotions about what you remember.
- Forgive yourself and others; permit yourself to move on.

130 | Make Peace with Everyone

When you forgive, you in no way change the past—but you sure do change the future.

Bernard Meltzer

Like instant gratification, holding a grudge gives you a little reward today, but it is at the expense of your future. Conversely, forgiving brings bigger future benefits but requires some sacrifice today.

The act of forgiving can help you improve your emotional control; you're no longer stuck in a negative emotional loop. The starting point of forgiveness is identifying your hurt and acknowledging your hurtful emotions. Then, by finding joy in the present you'll stop reliving the past.

Forgive Yourself | 131

> *The best way to start again is to ignore your past and forgive yourself.*

Moustafa Kadous

Empathy, compassion, kindness, and understanding are essential requirements you'll need to forgive yourself. Also, you must accept that forgiveness is a choice. Forgiveness is crucial to your healing process; it allows you to let go of any negative feelings you may be experiencing and move on.

So, identify the feeling, and give it a voice. Then, come to terms with the fact that mistakes are inevitable. Then, you can start experiencing the freedom that comes with forgiveness.

132 | Maintain Life Balance

> *Burnout is about resentment. Preventing it is about knowing yourself well enough to know what it is you're giving up that makes you resentful.*
>
> — *Marissa Mayer*

Self-care involves a reduction in burnout, a creation of sustainable work-life balance and engaging in the right behaviors and mindset. When others ask too much of you, be firm in your resolve to say "no." It is an important act of self-care.

Try these ways to include self-care in your daily routines:

- Analyze your daily routine to be sure that you have been getting enough sleep, eating a balanced diet, and exercising properly, especially when you start experiencing stress.

- Find a place to release your frustrations. Dancing, running or journaling are ways to air out your frustrations without hurting another person or yourself.

- Create a structure but be flexible about it. It will motivate you, create less distraction for you, and help you avoid getting things done in a rush.

- Minimize your money stress. Don't let your finances overwhelm you. Have a clear idea of your income sources and budget accordingly.

- Understand your feelings without judgment or attachment.

- Sit still, and rest.

133 | Do Not Get Affected by Social Media

> *No one posts their failures on social media; so, accept all their posts as is.*
>
> Moustafa Kadous

Are you always on the hunt for a social media dopamine pump? For example, how many likes and comments did my last post get? The truth is you need to stop looking at social media for a feeling of importance from other people.

Your best solution is to control and manage the amount of time you spend on social media. Do not let a digital platform deteriorate the single most valuable asset you have – time.

Tune in to Your Body and Mental State | 134

> *Alternating periods of activity and rest are a necessity to survive and to thrive. Plan accordingly.*

Tim Ferriss

On the journey to unlocking the best in you, one of the biggest lessons you'll discover is the importance of being flexible and self-compassionate. It is normal for your energy or productivity levels to fluctuate. But your plans aren't set in stone. If your current mental state can't accommodate certain actions and choices, change your plans accordingly, just don't change your goals.

Whenever you feel a genuine need to rest, do so guilt-free. Always tune in to your body and mental state. The world doesn't rest on your shoulders; don't act like it does.

135 | Work Effectively in a Team

> *Great things in business are never done by one person. They're done by a team of people.*
>
> *Steve Jobs*

A teamwork environment can provide dynamic and interesting work experiences to generate exceptional results, when in a team, appreciate the creativity and insight of others. Also, contribute 100 percent, especially when there are overlaps of roles and responsibilities and when there's need to advance the team's initiatives. For common goals and objectives, ensure that you are on the same page with your team members.

Make Flexible Plans | 136

> *Change the plan to achieve the goal, but don't change the goal itself.*

Moustafa Kadous

Goals can be flexible., Flexibility means you know your exact goals, but the path to achieving them is not carved in stone. This flexibility can protect you when you move too fast or too aggressively.

Plan with flexibility by having specific goals, making short-term plans (not more than three months), and trusting your team or yourself (when the plan is strictly for you).

137 | Peace in Your Heart

> *Nobody can bring you peace but yourself.*
>
> *Ralph Waldo Emerson*

Peace is part of your being and not what happens to you. Your peace is a choice. When you choose to have peace in your heart, no one can take it away from you even when turmoil, noise, and confusion surround you. True peace will elude you when you're in constant pursuit of fleeting, shallow, frivolous things.

Choose peace by investing yourself in genuine values that last. Imagine the kind of power you'll feel knowing that you can always choose to live each day with a peaceful heart.

Let Your Winners Run | 138

> *Cut your losses short and let your winners run.*

A Wall Street Saying

Instead of acquiring gains, people tend to avoid equivalent losses due to the loss aversion. Rather than cutting short and redirecting your attention to activities that produce better results, you're investing your time and energy into a failed project.

Ask yourself if it's the best use of your time to keep at a failed project because of what you've already invested in it. If not, consider the losses as a learning experience and move on; there are better things you can do with your time.

139 | Deploy Self-Massage

> *It's not selfish to love yourself, take care of yourself and make your happiness a priority; it is necessary.*
>
> *Mandy Hale*

If your body is constantly tense, you will struggle to focus on work and stay on top of your game. You can eliminate chronic pain by spending several weeks to address your most painful trigger points. While you must suffer some temporary discomfort, it comes with a bigger reward.

Self-massage can be a useful exercise for unlocking the best you. One of your best investments is to buy an inexpensive lacrosse ball or a foam roller. The thirty bucks you will spend on a self-massage tool would be like a drop in the ocean compared to your improved self-discipline, increased mobility, and eliminated or reduced pain.

Practice Self-Empathy | 140

> ...we all have empathy. We may not have enough courage to display it.

Maya Angelou

Practicing self-empathy is one thing that can change your life more than others. Self-empathy is an essential requirement for self-metta, or kindness towards yourself. One way to practice self-empathy is to take care of your body. Taking care of your body is anything that feels right and necessary for you.

141 | The Deadening of the Soul

> If you're prosperous in your soul, you'll be prosperous in whole, regardless of how many and how much physical possessions you have.
>
> *Mark Victor Hansen*

Curiously, most people rarely spend anything to improve themselves on the inside, but don't mind spending countless cash to improve their appearance through various treatments. Compare your cost, in time and money, of developing your inner self with the cost of improving your external appearance. Make sure the proportion is balanced every time.

Don't Let Others' Expectations Define Your Life | 142

> *Self-expectations give inspiration.*
> *Expectations from others hurt.*

Moustafa Kadous

Some of us make decisions based on how others expect us to perform so that we can gain their respect or appreciation. But people's expectations are theirs, and you have no obligation to fulfill them. Pushy influence usually leads to disappointment.

Removing expectations means letting go of unnecessary pressure. It doesn't mean you should lower your bar. You can only give your best when you feel relaxed.

143 | Protect Yourself from Burnout

> *Almost everything will work again if you unplug it for a few minutes.*
>
> *Anne Lamott*

When you are very motivated, you can easily burnout. Observe yourself and take time to rest once you notice any signs of tiredness. For optimal results, include a period of relaxation and fun time in your weekly routine.

Try these simple tips:

- Close your eyes and focus on one thing for five minutes.
- Take deep breaths or meditate.
- Switch locations.
- Work alone and with a team.
- Switch between creative and logical tasks frequently.
- Do something physical and still.

Have a Place to Call Home | 144

Happiness in a home is more important than the bigness of the house.

Moustafa Kadous

A home is any place where you enjoy love and happiness, feel safe and comfortable to unburden all your emotions. When you feel comfortable and safe, you gain a mental clarity that allows you to live out your full potential and be at your best.

Home is also a place where you and your loved ones can pull each other through rough times.

Start creating the conditions of a home in your house today, including features that give you satisfaction and peace of mind.

145 | Basic Health

> *Take care of your body. It's the only place you have to live in.*
>
> *Jim Rohn*

Care for your body like the maintenance of an expensive car, and it will perform perfectly and durably. Here are some basics:

- Make healthy food choices often. Your energy and ability to perform largely depends on what you eat.
- Don't put off going to the doctor until you've broken down completely; consult your doctor when you're sick. Also, take appropriate precautions; watch out for irregular or erratic body experiences; take appropriate vitamins, and go for regular check-ups.
- Wear clothes that make you feel attractive and confident.

Stop Robbing Your Future Self | 146

> *Every time you borrow money; you're robbing your future self.*

Nathan W. Morris

Don't disable your future self from using money. Rather, disable your current self from buying unimportant items, and you will save your future self. Once you've built up your savings, you can always borrow money from yourself without paying any interest rate. Taking this step is one of the keys to achieving financial freedom. No matter the coolness of the bonus points from credit card loans, stay clear of them!

147 | Be a More Patient Person

> *He that can have patience can have what he will.*
>
> *Benjamin Franklin*

Making yourself wait is a great way to practice patience. Start with small actions like waiting for a few minutes before opening that can of soda.

With more practice, you can move on to something bigger and gain more patience. Also, find time to decompress every day. You can relax and take deep breaths or take a walk to clear your head.

Cultivate Physical Excellence | 148

> *For in everything that men do, the body is useful; and in all uses of the body, it is of great importance to be in the best state of physical efficiency...a sound and healthy body is strong protection to a man.*

Socrates

An unhealthy body is an unhealthy mind. If you are constantly getting sick, your routine is out of the window, and it might take considerable time before you can get back into it.

Once you start exercising, your mental state will reflect the positive changes to your body. Now is the time to include a proper health and fitness regime into your routine.

149 | Get Rid of Virtue Vices

> *Most vices pretend as virtues and take advantage of this assumed resemblance.*
>
> Jean De La Bruyere

Some bad habits mask as virtues which makes them harder to eliminate. For example, those who jump from one business idea to another might claim that they are trying out different things until they find the perfect idea. But in reality, what they lack is the self-discipline to focus.

Critically analyze your deeply-held beliefs and be sure that they are not masquerading as a friend who gives you one dollar with one hand and collects five dollars from your wallet with the other hand.

Offering of Love | 150

> *Love is not only something you feel, it is something you do.*

David Wilkerson

Instead of reacting to frustration automatically, choose to find fulfillment in working through the complications. Don't poison your attitude with resentment; identify the value in the challenges.

Offer your best — especially your love — in the value you create. Spend all your irreplaceable work time very well. It should be an offering of love.

151 | Take A Break

> *Your ability to generate power is directly proportional to your ability to relax.*
>
> David Allen

Most times, you will get your best ideas when you are not even putting in the effort. Relax your brain for a specific period regularly to sharpen your focus and make sense of the things that come into your mind and space. Balance your life, work, and spirit; it will give you a focused intention and relaxed serendipity to support each other.

Listen to Your Heart | 152

> *Always listen to your heart; though it's on your left side, it's always right.*

Nicholas Sparks

Listen to your heart and heed to its instructions. Your effectiveness becomes evident when you work towards values that are of great importance to you. Then, you'll know how to choose the right actions or decisions over the wrong ones.

Despite the importance of your thoughts and actions, they are more driven by your true person. You are not a machine; you are intelligent, capable, flexible, and smart. You know joy; you can hope, feel, and love. Align your efforts with these feelings from your heart, and you will achieve truly remarkable results.

Chapter Six

PERSISTENCE

Daily tips to keep going without giving up till you achieve your goal.

> "Failing forward is the ability to get back up after you have been knocked down. Learn from your mistake and move forward in a better direction."
>
> John Maxwell

153 | Insist, Persist and Never Give Up

> *You are not a failure. You only need more persistence to reach your goals.*
>
> Moustafa Kadous

Thomas Edison is the epitome of persistence and never giving up. Anything worthwhile requires persistence. When you give up on what's important to you, then you might establish a pattern of giving up when things don't go according to your plan.

Always tell yourself that you are not a failure. It's only your actions that fail when you fall short of a particular goal. Here are three proven tips to master the art of never giving up:

- Pause to regain your composure when things aren't going as planned. Then, proceed and try again.
- Be honest with yourself especially when you fail. Admit and understand your mistakes. Then, channel all efforts to make amends.
- Focus on the good things especially when you are surrounded by chaos.

Constant Movement Is Key | 154

> *Dance to the beat of your drum; whether the world likes your rhythmic movements or not.*

Matshona Dhliwayo

Since humans are wired to be on a constant mission to improve our lives, constant movement is one of the keys to a successful life. If your progress is slow, you might feel the need to give up working on such a goal. However, by giving up, you can't accomplish your objectives. Therefore, it makes no sense to give up.

What you can do is to appreciate the little progress you are making daily, knowing fully well that it will eventually lead to you accomplishing your big goal.

155 | A Simple Adherence Trick

> *Those who use food diaries lose three times as much weight as those who don't.*
>
> *Tim Ferris*

If you want to be more aware of what you consume, take pictures of what you eat. A picture is irrefutable proof that you failed to stick with your resolutions. Since you know there is a consequence, you will pause and think before you cheat.

You can also use this trick to achieve other goals. For example, if you want to save more money, take pictures of all your purchases. Then, sort the ones that aren't a necessity.

Continue Working | 156

The harder you work for something, the greater you'll feel when you finally achieve it.

Deepraj Srivastav

Keep working at life because life becomes more fulfilling as you put more work into it. Life becomes more interesting when you can keep improving yourself. Let each challenge you face add purpose and strength to your experience. Take advantage of the opportunity in each day to make true progress in a world where things do go wrong.

157 | Channel Frustration into Energy

> *You should only compete with yourself ever. There is no fairer match.*
>
> *Todd Ruthman*

The energy you feel when you're frustrated is powerful. Instead of directing this energy in a negative direction, you can channel it positively. Since frustration is a feeling, you can reframe it from an irritant to a teacher. Use it to investigate what truly goes on inside you. Then, you can discover a deeper truth.

When you face this truth directly, it dissipates the energy in the feeling; it creates a space inside you so that you can choose what next to do.

Change Isn't Always Convenient | 158

> *Change is not made without inconvenience.*

Richard Hooker

I am sure that you expect and accept the inconveniences that come from remodeling your house. Since you want your house to be nice and cozy, you accept these conditions. Similarly, expect and accept the mess that often occurs as you make changes in your life, replacing the old with the new.

Always remember that both minor and major annoyances are part of the path going from worse to better. You should never give up or be frustrated by the inconveniences in the change process.

159 | Repel Negativity

> *I use haters as my motivators.*
>
> Moustafa Kadous

It's a fact; you'll have haters for doing something worthwhile. Some people will criticize you for anything and for various reasons.

Don't allow their negativity to lower your self-esteem or make you doubt yourself. A foolproof way to deal with haters is to ignore their insults or malice and focus only on yourself.

HATERS ARE MY MOTIVATORS

Handle Interruptions in Your Routine | 162

Circumstances may cause interruptions and delays, but never lose sight of your goal.

Mario Andretti

Follow the same routine when you travel as you follow when you are at home. Plan for situations that may likely disrupt your routine by developing a modified routine for such special circumstances. While this modified routine won't be as effective as your normal routine, it prevents you from losing focus or discipline.

163 | Have High Expectations of Yourself

> *High expectations are the key to everything.*
>
> Sam Walton

If you don't aim high, you might not achieve it. So, why not aim higher? When you set high expectations for yourself, you'll make yourself accountable to a higher standard. As a result, you won't give up until you've achieved it.

Start today. Set high expectations regarding your goals, both in the short-term and long-term.

However, don't let your high expectations put you under such enormous pressure that you crumble under the weight of the pressure.

165 | When Should You Stop Trying?

Try and fail but don't fail to try.

Stephen Kaggwa

If you haven't done something before, try doing it three times. The first time is to get over your fear of doing it. The second time is to learn how to do it, learning especially from your mistakes. The third time is to determine whether you like it. However, if you what you are doing doesn't align with your life goals or it's affecting your health negatively, stop it immediately.

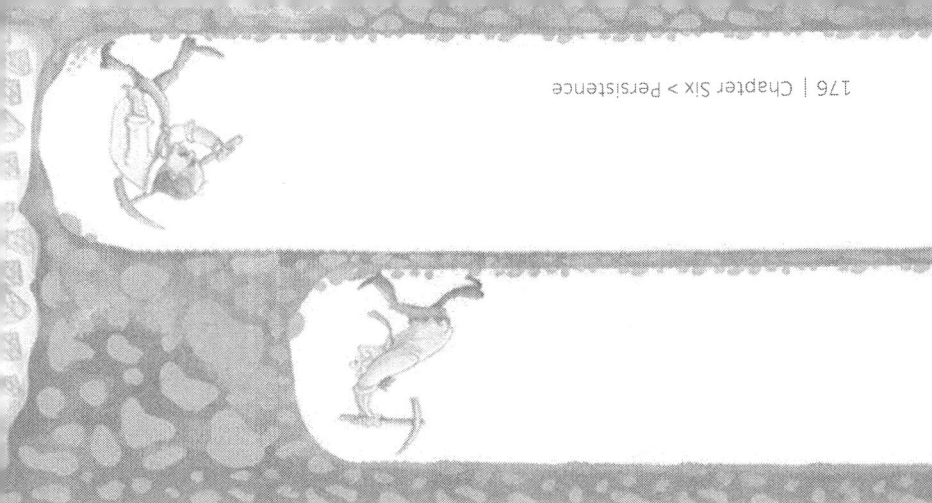

Resist the Temptation to Fight

> *Every moment of resistance to temptation is a victory.*
>
> Frederick William Faber

Anger is arguably the most common emotion. For some people, the urge to express their anger when they are attacked is so overwhelming that anger has become a reflex action. Your ability to control your anger can strengthen your impulse control and unlock the best in you.

Use these three tips to resist the temptation to fight when you are attacked:

- Walk away from the situation.
- Deflect the attack. For example, smile and thank the attacker.
- Find a funny side to the situation.

Make the Effort Count | 168

> *Average effort = average results;*
> *great effort = great results.*

Joe Whitbread

Doing a little less than necessary is the most tragic waste of effort. When you stop just short of the finish line, all your previous efforts up to that point count for nothing. In fact, a sign that you are getting closer to your goals is the fast pace of obstacles and challenges that start hitting you.

Seek to do a bit more. It is better to miss the mark on the side of accomplishment than on the side of failure. Keep going. Don't slow down until you exceed your goal.

169 | Make a Choice

> *Your life will only change when you choose to take a chance.*
>
> *Moustafa Kadous*

Unless you allow it to continue, nothing continues about you. You decide how you want your future to be and how you can act in it. When you disappoint yourself, don't allow the disappointing behavior to keep going on. Let go of what created regret and dismay and build upon what has served you.

Breathe new life into your world, your dreams, and most importantly, yourself.

Start today; don't delay.

A Positive Light | 170

> *Shine your light and make a positive impact on the world; there is nothing so honorable as helping improve the lives of others.*

Roy T. Bennett

Shine a positive light:

- On life and your life's experience will be filled with true richness.
- On the moments in each day and you'll find real treasure along every direction.
- On things out of your control and you will find several other ways to accomplish your goal.

171 | Unbendable Vision

> *Create the highest, grandest vision possible for your life, because you become what you believe.*
>
> *Oprah Winfrey*

Don't let a bad or difficult situation limit your thoughts, efforts, attitude, enthusiasm, or expectations. You are a person who can develop a rich and meaningful life out of your challenges and skills. Unleash the full power of your thoughts and imagination into positive, effective actions.

Despite your victories or defeats, you can make new choices at every point in time. Always carry a positive, firm vision within you. Channel the beauty of that vision to create good things for your life regardless of the situation.

Finish Strong | 172

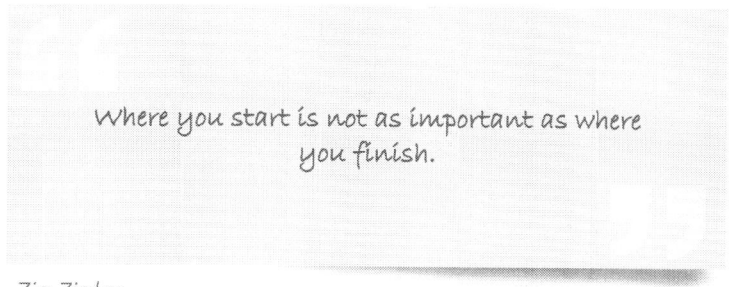

> *Where you start is not as important as where you finish.*

Zig Ziglar

The person who wins the race speeds up the pace when the finish line is near. When your challenges become more difficult, become more determined with your winning response. Remember why you're doing what you are doing, and you can start strong, stay strong, and finish strong.

173 | Your Memory

> "Remember why you started, remember where you're headed, think of how great it will be to get there, and keep going."

Ralph Marston

Your memory of what happened is your interpretation of what happened and its meaning to you; it's not what happened. The experience was never objective from the day you remembered it, and your recollection will be less objective with time. Each time you reflect on a memory, it can and will change.

From today, let your memories push you to a bright and meaningful life that's more than your imagination.

Stay with Your Problems for a Good While | 174

I think there's great beauty to having problems. That's one of the ways we learn.

Herbie Hancock

When next you face a problem, figure it out by yourself before seeking help. Keep in mind that this doesn't include life or death situations. If you're learning a new skill and can't figure out a step, go through your training content to figure it out.
Only seek assistance from your trainer when you still can't figure it out.

An excellent self-control practice is to reject the impulse to seek help immediately. Though you might expend a few extra minutes or hours to solve the problem, you will gain a new experience, become more patient, and develop more trust in your abilities.

Chapter Seven

PLANS & VISUALIZATION

Use these daily tips to make concrete plans and implement them.

> "The best thing about the future is that it only comes one day at a time."
>
> — Abraham Lincoln

175 | Start from the Other Direction

> *Visualize who you want to be, then work for it.*
>
> — *Gymaholic*

Follow this advice, and you can overcome your frustration of discovering the first step and spinning your wheels. So, imagine you've already achieved your goal. Now ask yourself what you did to achieve the goal; what you avoided to achieve it, and what you still need to do despite achieving the goal. Break the answers to these questions into small parts, and you will have created a list of actions that will lead you to your destination. Start with an action you can accomplish with ease, and continue from there.

Having a mental picture of each step of your journey toward making changes in your life can be just the motivation you need to get started.

Visualize with A Purpose | 176

> *Visualization is daydreaming with a purpose.*

Bo Bennett

Daydreaming helps your mind think about the goals you hope to achieve. However, this type of daydreaming should serve a purpose, which is how visualization differs from daydreaming.

Visualize a well-detailed and clear image of any goal you want to achieve. Imagine. Actually, see yourself achieving the goal you seek perfectly and completely. Be positive about this purpose and aim your actions to achieve the goals.

177 | Someday and Today

> *Work like a beast today to create a better tomorrow for yourself and your loved ones.*
>
> *Moustafa Kadous*

The choices you make, the way you live right now will determine the good things this moment will add to all the moments of your life. Today, you have a chance to:

- Fulfill a future wish of doing more than you are currently doing.
- Offer kindness and encouragement.

Don't be sorry because you missed out on these opportunities today.

Project A Positive Self-Image | 178

> *The picture you hold of yourself on the inside will reflect your behavior consistently.*

Brian Tracy

Make sure that the image you have of yourself matches your actions. A positive self-image creates a virtuous cycle, while a negative self-image prevents you from making the right changes. A positive self-image helps you to make the change you desire. If you believe deep down that you're productive, you'll feel good when you manifest that productivity in the real world.

Start with your self-image when you set your new goals. Rather than call yourself a failure, call yourself a person with vast experience and deep insights. It will be easier for you to stick with your goals when you change your opinion about yourself.

179 | A Gift to Yourself

> *Believe you can and you will.*
>
> — *Moustafa Kadous*

Challenge yourself today. See it as a gift to yourself. Choose a new task or goal for the day and challenge yourself to accomplish it before the day is over. Let it be something that pushes you and inspires you. Then, when you look back on this day, you will appreciate your decision to achieve this valuable accomplishment.

Now, get busy to make it happen. Create a practical plan that can help you to accomplish that set goal.

Once you reach that goal, pause briefly and fully savor the fulfillment that comes with the experience. The side benefit to accomplishing this goal is that you will feel more confident to set new challenges and accomplish them.

Create New Habits with the Habit Loop | 180

> *Empower your new routines by breaking your more ingrained habits one step at a time.*

Moustafa Kadous

A habit loop can include a reward, a routine (action), and a cue (a signal to perform a habit) for engaging in a habit. This loop creates an automatic behavior for you when you perform it repeatedly. With more empowering routines, you can use this loop to replace bad habits.

For example, rather than having a few drinks with your co-workers after a long day, convincing them to do yoga with you is a better alternative. Your cue is the long tiring day, your reward is the social time and relaxation. That quick yoga routine is a healthier way to refresh your body's energy.

You can trigger a new habit in three ways. But you don't have to combine all three ways at the same time. The cue you'll choose depends on the habit you intend to develop.

Cue 1

Time-based cues: This helps you to stick with routines repeatedly. Choose a date and time to perform a specific activity and stick with this schedule regardless of your feelings.

Cue 2

Location: Use the same location for your routine. Then, when you don't feel like performing the activity, your familiarity with the location helps you overcome your resistance.

Cue 3

Preceding event: For example, start a daily gratitude habit during a specific period of your day. You can easily build this habit into your life by making it as small as possible.

The secret to the choice of a successful cue is to pick a specific trigger that you can act upon immediately.

Demolish the Bridges Behind You | 181

> *I demolish the bridges behind me.... Then, there is no choice but to move forward.*

Fridtjof Nansen

Suppose you are working toward a goal but you keep your safety net fully in place beneath you. That comfort zone can make you lazy. that you will accomplish the goal makes lazy.

The better option is to destroy the safety net, make it almost impossible for you to lose. Before you do that, however, consider all necessary risks that you may face without the safety net.

For example, quitting your job to start a business when you are the breadwinner of your family might not be a good idea. Make calculated risks. Shed the safety net. You will never be ready, and there will never be a perfect moment. So, start now.

182 | Embark on New Adventures

> *The biggest adventure you can ever take is to live the life of your dreams.*
>
> *Oprah Winfrey*

Though crossing the ocean in a kayak, trekking the Himalayas, or any other travel experiences are certainly adventures, mixing up your everyday routine can also create simple and novel experiences. For example, drive a new route during your morning commute and on your way home. Do anything outside your comfort zone, decline your routine requests and accept requests you usually reject.

Get ready for surprises!

Make Long-Term Commitments | 183

> *When long-term commitment is combined with high levels of practice, skills skyrocket.*

Daniel Coyle.

In a moment of extreme desire, it is natural to become fully focused on the task ahead. However, that clear sense of focus can begin to fade as the emotion of the moment starts to subside. For you to achieve great things, you must learn how to constantly maintain and intensify a clear and driving focus over the long-term.

Seek to truly understand who you are, especially why you desire those things you desire. Keep asking till you find an answer that aligns with your true personality. Then, connect this true personality with what you desire and that growing focus till the goals you desire become a part of you.

184 | Don't Follow Someone Else's Plan

> *If you're struggling to execute the plans that lead to your goals, reevaluate your goals immediately; they might be someone else's goals, not yours.*
>
> *Moustafa Kadous*

If you find it extremely difficult to follow the plans toward achieving your goals, then you need to reevaluate whether they are truly your goals or someone else's goals. Ask yourself some soul-searching questions. For example, are you a doctor by choice or parental plan? Is your desire to achieve a particular goal your idea or societal expectation?

As you keep your dreams in mind, discard any plan that doesn't align with your values and personality. Create and follow your plans only.

Review Your Path Periodically

> *Travelers, there is no path; paths are made by walking.*

Antonio Machado

A path is a tool, and it's only useful so long as it gets you closer to your goals. There will come a time when you have to leave a path. The best way to decide to stay or leave a path is to be rid yourself of negative feelings. Put yourself in a neutral state of mind and review your path. I suggest you do so periodically.

Analyze your strategy to be sure that it's still delivering results and still feels right to you. Ask yourself whether this path can still deliver the results you desire for another month, quarter, or year. Like any other tool, you might need to change paths at one time or another.

186 | The How Is as Important as the Outcome

> *Learn by doing. The theory is nice, but nothing replaces experience.*
>
> *Tony Hsieh*

There is a process for attaining every goal.

You will miss out on the personal growth experience of the journey when you compromise the process by cutting corners. In your quest to achieve your dreams very quickly, don't hurt anyone, cheat, compromise your moral principles, or cut corners. The bragging rights of your accomplishments aren't worth giving up your peace of mind.

Know the Best Time to Work on Your Highest Priorities | 187

> *You have to decide your priorities and dare to say 'no' to other things. And the way you do that is by having a bigger 'yes' burning inside.*

Stephen R. Covey

Find and use the times when you feel mentally alert and excited for tasks involving critical decisions, complex thoughts, and problem-solving. When you are not as focused and engaged, perform less complex, unimportant, and routine tasks.

Pick three consecutive days and track how you spend each day. Record what you accomplished within each hour and rank the accomplishments as it relates to your productivity. Then, you can organize your days around your energy and not your time.

188 | Make Your Plans Specific, Quantifiable and Repeatable

> *She turned her 'can'ts' into 'can's' and her dreams into plans.*
>
> *Kobi Yamada*

When you make your plans specific, each day's action should get you closer to goals. If, by your nature, it is difficult to tell whether or when you've accomplished a goal, then you need to set specific, quantifiable sub-goals. Then, you can have proof that you've improved your abilities or skills based on the efforts you've exerted so far.

Keep in mind that the real work starts after you've taken the first action that brings you closer to your goals.

Create Systems

> *80% of your problems are not people problems... they are system problems because systems create the behaviors of people.*

Andy Stanley

Most people assume that temptations are similar to a knight defending his kingdom against the invader.

The best way to avoid temptations is to protect yourself against them. Preparation is more valuable than self-control. Put up roadblocks ahead of time, it will prepare you for difficult situations even when your resolve isn't being tested.

Analyze and understand your various strengths and weaknesses to create a personalized system that can help you to achieve your goals.

190 | Keep Your Business Self-Sustaining

> *I built a system simple enough to sustain itself.*
>
> *Pierre Omidyar*

There is no such thing as a static business that can be self-sustaining in this age of constant market evolution and new technology. These days, being self-sustaining involves taking frequent and aggressive measures to stay ahead of the competition before you start feeling the pain of new competitors around you.

The reality is, you can't stop improving your business and expect it to be self-sustaining.

You must make actual efforts and be disciplined to implement a plan of regular strategic acquisitions and redefine your product to reach new levels.

Consider Tony Robbins' model for success, CANI, an acronym for "Continuous and Never-ending Improvements." Make your plan for regular change a priority.

Self-Awareness Is a Key to Self-Mastery | 191

> *Self-awareness and self-judgment are not the same. Self-awareness is looking, seeing, and discovering your true self.*

Moustafa Kadous

Self-awareness is key to making any change.

It is by paying attention to your actions that you can be sure you are living up to your ideals.

Review your actions for each previous week to identify any of your actions that didn't fit your goals, values, and ideals. Then, make appropriate changes and keep up this routine to keep improving your life.

192 | Develop Routines to Overcome a Bad Mood

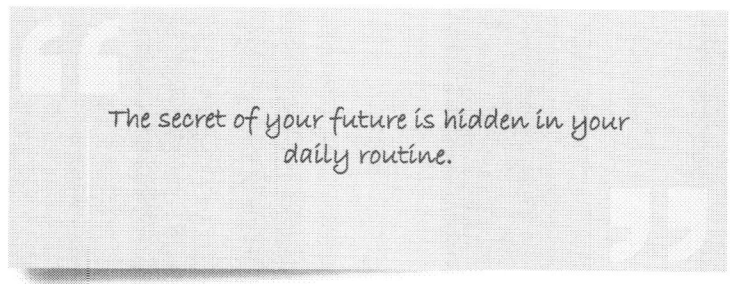

> *The secret of your future is hidden in your daily routine.*
>
> Mike Murdock

Naturally, there will be times when you will be in a bad mood. Without an established routine, waking up in a bad mood can ruin your day, even so far that you could discard your current resolutions for the remaining part of the day. Establish a daily routine and instill it in your mind such that it is almost impossible for you not to perform it even when you're having a bad day.

Personal Routine. | 193

> *Routines are the ideal way to bookend your day... they are the building blocks of effectiveness, efficiency and efficacy.*

Mike Vardy

The effectiveness of a routine lies in developing one that suits your personality, not by following someone else's specific routine. Develop routines, at least three, to improve your control over the day and eliminate indecision.

For example:

- Set routines for waking up and going to bed. Your weekly schedule becomes predictable and makes you more productive.
- Set morning routines to have a good start to the day.
- Set work routines, especially when you have a flexible work schedule.

194 | Don't Be Afraid of the Future

> *Your future can be better than your visualization even if the past didn't happen the way you envisioned it.*
>
> *Moustafa Kadous*

Are you so scared of the future that you think it is going to attack you and stab you in the back? Rather than being scared of the future, consider it a challenge, a compelling story, or a pleasant surprise that's about to unfold.

If you're scared of tomorrow, think only about today, how you can go through it and make it better. The best way to prepare for tomorrow is to make today count.

Create a Vivid Mental Image of Your Goals | 195

> *You have to work hard to get your thinking clean and make it simple. Once you get there, you can move mountains.*

Steve Jobs

Decide on an end goal. Then, write down realistic and descriptive steps you need to reach the larger goal. Focus on the observable changes, for example, research all relevant certifications and registering for the exam before the year ends, along with the consequent inner ones, such as a pay raise and an improved life.

Use affirmations, a success-oriented language, stated in the present tense, not the future tense.

For example, instead of 'I will receive a pay rise when I get my certifications', the best statement would be, "I have my certifications, and I have a pay raise."

196 | Turn the Page and Look to the Future

> I don't think of the past. The only thing that matters is the everlasting present.

Laura Moncur

Answer this question with all honesty, "What success have you had from using your past story as an excuse for your current life?" Focusing only on your past mistakes will reinforce the belief that you are a victim, and it will affect your chances of success in life.

Your best option is to turn the page and create the future you desire.

Find the Motivation to Move Forward | 197

> I try to see my troubles in their proper perspective. I say to myself: 'two months from now, I shall not worry about this bad break. So, why worry about it now?' Why not assume the same attitude that I will have in two months from now?

William L. Phelps

Are you struggling or worrying about getting to the end of a goal? Visualize yourself accomplishing the goal. If it takes a few days or weeks to eventually accomplish the goal, would you find the motivation to move forward?

Even if it'll take you a few months to accomplish the goal, worrying about it is counter-productive since the discomfort is a temporary condition.

198 | Hardships Can Write Your Life Story in a Positive Way

> When you struggle a lot to accomplish something, the kind of joy you'll feel when you finally accomplish it is indescribable.

Moustafa Kadous

Each time you struggle with your goal and feel like giving up, remind yourself that the hardships make your life story exciting and memorable. Use your current hardships to embrace your human nature and grow as a person. Then, you can share your awesome inspirational story with others in the future.

Accept It | 199

> *When you accept yourself, the whole world accepts you.*

Lao Tzu

You will create real value and experience great peace in acceptance when you're not overwhelmed by trying to prove yourself. Though it might be necessary to fight against some issues, you can simply accept them. Then, you can enable yourself to move forward quickly.

Free yourself to make the best of useless battles by accepting what has happened and not fighting against another point of view.

200 | Feel It

> *Whatever you believe with feeling becomes your reality.*
>
> *Brian Tracy*

Feel the way you'd like to feel today and about today. The feelings of joy, power, efficiency, and purpose have no specific set of conditions. Feel your expected experience before you have it. Then, translate this feeling into actions and results.

Go ahead; feel the feelings that push you to optimal performance. It will help you make good things happen.

Chapter Eight

BELIEFS & MINDSET

Tips to critically analyze your mindset in the quest to achieve your goals.

> "Beliefs have the power to create and the power to destroy. Human beings have the awesome ability to take any experience of their lives and create a meaning that disempowers them or that can literally save their lives."
>
> — Tony Robbins

201 | Stay a Champion

> *To be a great champion you must believe you are the best. If you're not, pretend you are.*

Muhammad Ali

You don't just want to become a champion; you want to stay a champion. There will always be new goals to reach, new comfort zones to explore, and even little-by-little self-improvements to make.

So, embrace the idea that discomfort is a teacher. It will strengthen you and push you to achieve greater feats. Always remember that the top performers in the world still feel fear and experience discomfort.

Who You Are | 202

> *You are what you believe yourself to be.*

Paulo Coelho

What thoughts could replace those thoughts that hold you back? What factors would you work on to improve and make your current time and place a little better? What excuses would you no longer tolerate if you were being honest with yourself?
What would you do from now on to live the life of your dreams?

How you answer these questions make you who you are and who you can be.

203 | A Stronger Understanding of Your Personality

> *If you cannot get rid of the family skeleton, you may as well make it dance.*

George Bernard Shaw

Knowing your family history can give you a stronger understanding of your personality and motivate you to deepen your roots for generations to come. Consider it an act of altruistic selflessness to be aware of and have a greater sense of responsibility towards your progenitors and your future generation. Learning about your family history can help you identify patterns of surviving hard times and overcoming failures.

Make it a point to talk with someone in an older generation to learn about your family history.

Define Yourself by Multiple Roles | 204

> *Those who gain their sense of identity from many areas are more resilient when they fail in any other area.*

Neil Fiore

If you define yourself by a specific role, your self-image will be restricted to that role only. When you make mistakes in that role, you might struggle to find the inspiration to recover from those mistakes.

Conversely, if you define yourself by multiple roles and you fail in one domain, your performance in other domains will give you the inspiration to recover from the domain where you failed.

205 | Stop Assuming for Others

> We need to stop assuming things and start clarifying things. It makes life less complicated.

Marika Mattos

Asking, not assuming or even affirming statements, is the key to understanding others better. Try saying back what you heard the other person say so that you are sure both of you have a clear understanding of what the person is saying. Keep practicing this till you can stop the bad habit of "assuming" completely.

Positive Attributes of Pride | 206

> *It is normal to rise above pride, but you must have the pride to do so.*

Georges Bernanes

Pride can be a real asset provided you nurture its positive aspects and keep your ego in check. Don't go out of your way to seek praise or brag for doing something well. Be comfortable knowing that you are putting out your best work without needing anyone's validation.

Take a moment to do this simple self-reflection. Be honest with your answer to this question; Are you leaning toward selfishness with your level of pride?

207 | Create Your Life's Maxims

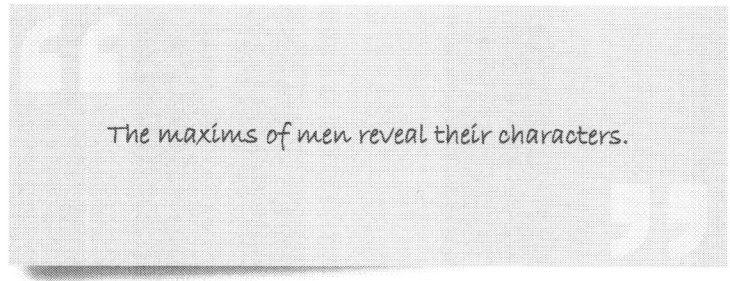

> *The maxims of men reveal their characters.*
>
> *Luc de Clapiers*

Always use empowering and positive maxims, they will reveal your character and make you successful.

List the most important truths you live by and analyze each of them to be sure that they improve you as a person. Replace the ones that don't make you a better person with the ones that will do.

Eliminate Psychological Limits | 208

> *Nothing is impossible. With so many people saying it couldn't be done, all it takes is an imagination.*

Michael Phelps

Our beliefs are stronger than our environment.

A wonderful way to show what's possible, which pushes your psychological limits, is to expose yourself to high performers. Reading stories of everyday people who've accomplished extraordinary success without any hidden advantages such as natural talent or resources is your proof that nothing is impossible. You only need to be open-minded and remove any psychological barrier in your head.

209 | Radiate Positive Energy

> *When success is your only option, positivity has to be your only choice.*
>
> *Germany Kent*

You'll feel better about yourself and your surroundings when you can project more positivity.

Each time you want to start believing your inner voice's negativity and pessimism, stop and write down your thoughts. The moment you've taken to slow down the momentum of your negative thoughts will help you to be more rational and clear-headed.

So, separate your negative thoughts from the facts. Rather than retrogress into a negative loop, you will move into a more positive frame of mind.

Habits as Shackles | 210

Don't let your habits become your handcuffs.

Elizabeth Berg

While habits are the key to improving your life, they can also be shackles that limit your life and choices to preselected routines. Is it a good habit to be highly productive and always work on achieving new goals? Absolutely. But you will miss out on valuable life experiences and even burn out when you don't take the time to relax.

As you form new habits, establish new rules around when you can forgo your habits for a temporary period.

211 | Mental Resilience Is Vital

> *...anything you lose comes around in another form.*
>
> *Jalaluddin Rumi*

When you've just experienced a loss such as a breakup or a business going bankrupt, it is hard to see any opportunity disguised in it. One way to move on is to remind yourself that your loss will come around in a different positive form. Perhaps, for example, the business' bankruptcy is to enable you to focus on a better idea by freeing up your resources.

Whenever you experience a loss, find the opportunities in it. It might be impossible for you to calm down enough to uncover any opportunity from bigger difficulties. So, start by uncovering opportunities in small negative events.

Review Your Most Habitual Thoughts | 212

> *He who controls his thoughts controls his destiny.*

Ross Arntson

One factor that affects your peace of mind is the quality of your thoughts. Healthy thoughts can lead to better health, higher happiness index, and more positive outcomes.

Improve the standard of your thoughts by stopping your thoughts about unnecessary things and not obsessing about monetary gains. Also, adopt a simple lifestyle; it reduces needless socio-economic issues.

213 | Avoid Generalizations

> *Generalizations are seldom if ever true and are usually utterly inaccurate.*
>
> *Agatha Christie*

Generalization is a characteristic of lazy thinking. If you want to unlock the best you, you have to disassociate yourself from lazy thinking. Assuming that a frequently repeated opinion is a fact is one of the most dangerous types of generalizations.

Be conscious enough to catch yourself proclaiming generalizations. You can only have an opinion when you can prove beyond a reasonable doubt that your opinions are based on facts.

Practice Smiling Often | 214

> *Better by far you should forget and smile*
> *than that you should remember and be sad.*

Christina Rossetti

Recall an event that made you smile and smile or imagine what's about to happen that can make you smile, then smile.

It can be something, pleasant, positive, and uplifting. It can be how someone special brightened your day or the glow on your children's face each time they see you. It can also be a gloriously beautiful day in the past week that made you feel great.

Smile as much as possible, it tunes you to the positive possibilities of life and you can make that wonder to work for you.

215 | Stop Trying to Be Like Everyone Else

> *Stop trying to be someone else. Just be yourself and wholeheartedly own that.*
>
> *Natalie Sisson*

You will miss out on all the things that will make you great when you desire to be someone else. It's fine to admire qualities, habits, or hobbies of another person. But be sure that you are admiring and developing these traits to improve yourself not to be *like* someone else.

Treat that person as a role model rather than be envious of him or her. Also, learn from their mistakes; they are human after all, and they are bound to make mistakes.

Stop and reflect on all things that are great about you.

Life Isn't So Bad After All | 216

> *Life's not so bad after all. There is not only poison but also antidotes.*

Irving Stone

Don't feel too bad about your current challenges or the fact that there seems to be no way around or over them. Feeling bad about your current situation only makes matters worse.

Instead of feeling bad, use that chance to shift your perspective by re-evaluating what matters to you. Through this new point of view, you will discover better ways to handle your current 'not-so-good' life experiences.

217 | Be the Example of Your Ideas

> *Example has more followers than reason.*
>
> Christian Nestell Boven

When people wonder why you're deliberately making your life difficult or laugh at your efforts, don't bother to reason with them. It won't work. Save your time and energy.

Your best option is to focus on your goals and set an example. When the results start flowing in, these people will understand why you do what you do and follow your example or keep quiet. Your goal is to set an example and not spend empty words.

Don't Feed Your Temper | 218

> *Keeping anger is similar to attempting to grab and throw a lump of hot coal at another person. It will burn your hands first.*

Moustafa Kadous

Anger, like any other emotion that results in impulsive decisions that you later regret, won't allow you to unlock the best you. Often, you can't prevent your anger from turning into full-blown rage. However, instead of feeding your anger, you can act quickly and suppress it.

The next time you feel anger, count the days you are able to suppress your first impulse to respond to that anger. It is one proven way to eliminate frequent anger attacks. After a 7-day winning streak, you should have made substantial progress.

Practicing how to be more patient is another proven way. Make conscious efforts not to feed your temper You will reduce the frequency of losing your temper and gain better emotional control.

219 | Your Thoughts Define Your Abilities

> *Believe in yourself and you will be unstoppable.*

Emily Guay | W. Michael Scott

The reverse is also true; if you think you can't, then you won't. Even when you try, you will fail because you've defeated yourself mentally before you even get started.

When next you find yourself in a situation where you have a low chance of success, believe you will overcome it and act as you have overcome it. While it won't always work because life isn't a fairy tale, you're putting yourself at a great advantage by taking action without hesitation.

Stop Wishing, Start Believing | 220

> *Don't just wish for it; you must work towards it.*

Moustafa Kadous

Your language is an effective strategy that can help you to develop success-friendly habits, traits, and behaviors. Each time you use the words "I wish," you suppress your ability and confidence to accomplish your goals. Why? The words "I wish" is proof that you lack the belief that the goal is achievable.

Most times, it's not that you can't accomplish the goal. It's your brain projecting your limiting beliefs. Now, make a list of what you can transform from "I wish" to "Here's how I'm going to do it."

221 | Optimism Leads to Greater Achievement

> *Optimism is a happiness magnet. If you stay positive, good things and good people will be drawn to you.*
>
> *Mary Lou Retton*

One trait of unlocking the best in you is having a positive attitude. If you don't believe you will receive greater compensation in the future, there is no point in denying yourself instant gratification.

Take these steps to become more optimistic:

- Appreciate what you already have. If you're not happy with what you own today, you won't appreciate what you'll have tomorrow.

- Surround yourself with positive energy vibes. If you spend time with pessimistic grumblers and read or listen to fearful news, you'll struggle to express optimism.

Increase Your Self-Awareness | 222

> *Self-awareness allows you to make mistakes and learn from them.*

Moustafa Kadous

Self-awareness is the habit of paying careful attention to your thoughts, feelings, and behavior.
By being self-aware, you can align your ideals with your actions and raise your happiness levels. Also, you will recognize what you do well and what you need to do.

One way to increase your self-awareness is to practice regular mindfulness, practice of keeping your attention focused on the present moment. It will open your eyes to the way your mind thinks and help you realize that you are not your thoughts.

223 | Practice Professional Courage

> *In every success story, you will find someone who has made a courageous decision.*
>
> — Peter F. Drucker

If you are like most people, you are afraid of conflict in a work setting, especially when it seems that the conflict can impact your financial security and professional future. While conflict can be negative, it can also help you accomplish your work mission and personal vision. Conflict can be a positive thing at work when the people involved address it openly and in view of clear goals, positive communication, and respect for colleagues.

Stand up for principles or ideas that can help you create meaningful change, serve customers, and be more successful at your job.

Discard Stagnating Thoughts | 224

> *Change your thoughts and change your world.*

Norman Vincent Peale

Your feelings depend on your thoughts, and how you view your work depends on your feelings. While there will always be lots of thoughts in your head, you can focus on the ones you choose. Thoughts about trying new things, experimenting, and excitement will move you forward.

Use affirmations, positive phrases repeated often and daily, to get rid of stagnating thoughts.

If your affirmation is, "I am limitless," your chant would be the same words, but you could shout it while beating your chest and jumping around. It is a scientifically proven fact that our brain is more susceptible to reprogramming when it's in a state of heightened emotion.

225 | Stop Seeking Approval

> *Once you know who you are, being is enough. You feel neither superior to anyone nor inferior to anyone, and you do not need anyone's approval because you've awakened to your infinite worth.*

Deepak Chopra

Before you seek approval from others, pause and ask yourself, "What's my opinion about this matter?" Then ask, "Why can't I trust my opinion about it?" An important step in overcoming your need for approval is understanding your motive behind it.

Focus on what makes you happy and stop worrying about other people's opinions. True self-confidence begins when you accept all parts of yourself. As you accept who you are and know the truth about yourself, you will discover that you don't need others' approval or input anymore.

Ask Why

Ask 'why' five times about every matter.

Daiichi Ohno

By asking 'why' about any situation, thought, or loss many times you will get the root cause of what went wrong – what went right. It can help you to decide whether a choice aligns with your core values.

For example, suppose you want to take a job, here are the five "whys" to ask:

- Why should I take this job? The pay is good and I can grow my career.
- Why is that important? I don't want a string of meaningless jobs; I want to build a career.
- Why? I want to live a meaningful life.
- Why? I want to live a happy life.
- Why? A happy life is my utmost desire in life.

227 | Understand the Deeper Meanings Behind Your Temptations

> *Asking the proper questions can help you have a better understanding of your problematic behaviors.*

Moustafa Kadous

Seek a deeper meaning about your problematic behaviors and temptations by asking the following questions:

- Why do you use certain techniques to distract or comfort yourself?
- What's the motive behind distracting or comforting yourself?
- What are the triggers or emotional needs that result in those negative behaviors?
- What emotional payoffs are you expecting from engaging in those techniques?

Positive Emotions | 228

> *It is your responsibility to ensure that positive emotions constitute the dominating influence of your mind.*

Napoleon Hill

How you choose to feel is more important than how you used to feel. If you've felt distracted, discouraged, and weary, that's in the past. Instead, you can decide to feel focused, purposeful, enthusiastic, and energetic.

Act on these positive feelings to create the life of your dreams.

229 | In Its Own Time

> *Don't stop. You'll achieve your desires in due time.*
>
> — Moustafa Kadous

Let life come in its own time. Don't waste time in idleness or race ahead of life. Take the time to enjoy, think, and focus, and don't make emergencies out of non-emergencies.

It's a waste of energy to go fast just for the sake of it. You'll give yourself big anxiety trying to rush through each moment. Take time to enjoy the great treasures that will unfold in each beautiful day.

Allow | 230

> *You are allowed to be a masterpiece and a work in progress simultaneously.*

Sophia Bush

Give yourself permission. Allow:

- your mind to be creative, powerful, and peaceful.
- your words to be helpful, kind, comforting, and uplifting.
- yourself to imagine the way to build on life's greatness.
- yourself to have a clear and strong purpose.
- your actions to continue with focus and confidence.
- love to direct your intentions.
- goodness to fill your world and abundance to flow into your life.

231 | Disallow the Fear of Missing Out

> *That fear of missing out on things will make you miss out on everything.*
>
> *Etty Hillesum*

If you are worried about what you're missing, you won't fully experience what you're doing. Make a choice and give yourself to everything with enthusiasm and confidence and without regrets.

Don't be afraid of missing other activities, show gratitude that you can invest your time in the activities you have chosen, and the good things you own. Relax and let a total sense of satisfaction fill you up.

Chapter Nine

SUCCESS

Proven daily tips that can guide you to success.

> "The secret of success is learning how to use pain and pleasure instead of having pain and pleasure use you. If you do that, you're in control of your life. If you don't life controls you."
>
> — Tony Robbins

232 | Maintain the Success Spirit

> *The road to success is always under construction.*
>
> *Lily Tomlin*

Suppose you set a goal for yourself six months ago, and six months later you achieve the goal. There are proven ways to maintain that success so that you won't slack off and erase everything you've achieved so far.

- Commit yourself to excellence without seeking approval. Developing your sense of pride and accomplishment is better than a pat on the back from friends, family, or co-workers.
- Always assume your goal is a project that is always in progress. Don't stop learning. For example, if you want to advance your business, learn more about what successful people in your industry are doing.
- Make it your way of life to keep going the extra mile.

Remain Humble No Matter What | 233

> If you truly want to succeed (and remain successful), you have to stay humble because it can all go away in the blink of an eye.

Raven Goodwin

Rather than smugly sitting on your knowledge or bragging about, build on it. Learning more and truly listening more leads to more accomplishments. But genuine humility leads you to more satisfaction and inner peace.

Make good use of your achievements and find fulfillment by having a meaningful and positive effect on other people without looking for that stroke of ego.

234 | Help Without Any Strings Attached

> *Successful people constantly look for opportunities to help others. Unsuccessful people want to benefit from helping others.*
>
> *Brian Tracy*

When you sincerely help others, you feel an incomparable joy within you. Even if some people take advantage of your generosity, don't let that deter you from continuing to lift others. When you lift one person, at least two other people benefit from your kindness.

Regardless of your circumstance, personality, skills, or resources, you can make a positive difference in the lives of others. Open your mind to discover those ways and enjoy the feeling of a well-lived life. For example, share a book that helped you. It will help them learn, discover, and improve themselves.

Stretch Yourself | 235

> *[Sometimes], life begins at the end of your comfort zone.*

Neale Walsh

You grow and improve by attempting what you couldn't do previously. It's true; useful learning comes from understanding and mastering what's outside your limit. Constantly stretching yourself beyond your previous limitation is a path to achievement. What has held you back can be your springboard to success. If you don't leave your comfort zone, you'll remain stuck forever.

Consider all your previous progress; you will discover that reaching milestones came from you shaking off your limitations. Since you've done it before, you can do so today and repeatedly going forward.

236 | Pay the Price of Personal Growth

> *If you are not ready to pay the price of personal growth, you're not ready to grow.*
>
> *Moustafa Kadous*

On your journey towards improving your life, here are some things you can expect:

- Your immediate social circle being puzzled about why you are doing what you do to achieve a great today and an even greater tomorrow. You will be better off ignoring those voices.
- You might struggle to connect with some people in your life. You must prepare yourself for the reality that some of your relationships may not be as fulfilling as you'd expect.
- You will live a better life than most people who are either unhappy at work, broke, unhealthy, or obese. But don't feel guilty for making those better choices. Realize that you've earned the right to enjoy your current life.

However, in all that you do, never ignore your family. Family is life.

Learn to Love What You Do | 237

> *The only way to do great work is to love what you do.*

Steve Jobs

The work experience is one important factor in career contentment. Passion for your career comes with mastery and time; so, you need to be patient. Also, regardless of your field, remember that success is about quality. You need to do what is necessary to improve your work.

Focus on acquiring unique, sellable skills and refine the quality of what you do with the focus of a devoted craftsman. Then, you will build a new, rare, practical passion in your career based on mastery and commitment.

238 | Teach Others

> *Never miss an opportunity to teach; when you teach others, you teach yourself.*
>
> — *Itzhak Perlman*

When you teach others, you grow, expand, refine your communication skills, and deepen your understanding of the information you share. Dedicated teaching helps you build humility as you will realize that you are only an instrument through which knowledge flows.

You can get started teaching what you already know, and no, it doesn't have to be in a college and school environment. You can teach via YouTube, Udemy, Teachable, Thinkific, and other online teaching platforms.

Rejoice in Others' Successes | 239

I rejoice in the success of others, knowing that there is plenty for us all.

Louise Hay

When your competitive tendencies prevent you from rejoicing in the achievements of others, then you need to start re-evaluating your thought patterns. Fear and self-criticism form part of the reasons why we hesitate to celebrate the accomplishments of others.

Stop comparing your talents with that of other people and learn to see the inherent gifts that are unique to others. Celebrate and encourage the splendor of their gifts.

240 | Stop Passing the Buck

> *If you're passing the buck, don't ask for change.*
>
> *David Gerrold*

Passing the buck is also known as playing the blame game. It is the act of evading your responsibility of your choices or decisions by passing it to another person or group. When you constantly play this blame game, it is a sign of disinterest or disengagement.

One proven way to stop passing the buck is to empower yourself with the tools for success — a checklist of best practices that helps you stick to the grind and achieve success.

Rent Is Due Every Day | 241

> ...success is never owned. Success is only rented, and the rent is due every day.

Rory Vaden

One powerful way to look at success is through the rent metaphor. Rather than think that you have been given success -- which can make you complacent and take it for granted -- assume you rent success, and you have to keep paying the rent to keep it for life.

A side benefit of this viewpoint is that you'll no longer look for temporary solutions or shortcuts.

Each time you remember that you must pay rent every day, you will make sure that your actions affirm the success that you thoroughly deserve.

242 | Seek Help

> *The man who asks a question is a fool for a minute; the man who does not ask is a fool for life.*
>
> *Confucius*

It's fine to ask questions, just don't make it a regular occurrence. You need facts and not someone else's opinion to make a balanced decision. Someone else's decision is always going to be skewed based on their way of thinking and experience.

The next time you are unsure of your next step and need more information, undertake genuine research for yourself. Start with Google and not forums or boards.

Improve Other People | 243

> *We can't help everyone but everyone can help someone.*

Ronald Reagan

Look for several opportunities in each day for you to have a positive impact on the lives of those around you. When you enrich the lives of other people genuinely, you will discover your true richness. Regardless of your current realities, there are ways you can give of yourself to improve the world around you.

Offer kindness by lending a helping hand today. You will not only be lifting the lives of others, but you will also be lifting your life.

244 | Many Paths to Success

> *There are no secrets to success. It is the result of preparation, hard work, and learning from failure.*
>
> *Colin Powell*

You must create your path to success by yourself. No one else can make you happy, and no one can determine the best path for you when you want to create the best life you desire.

You need to fully understand your purpose and value, then implement a strategy to accomplish your dreams. In this way, you become more focused and can eliminate stress, frustration, confusion, and conflict that won't aid your path to success.

Develop a Success Attitude | 245

Your mindset defines life as good or bad.

Moustafa Kadous

When you develop both an attitude of success and an expectation for that success, combined with diligent work, you're certain to achieve your goals. The amount of effort it takes to come up with the reasons for your accomplishments is the same as coming with excuses.

Change your thoughts each time you start thinking that you're destined to fail and should just accept your misfortune. Come up with reasons why you will be successful and remind yourself of the reasons why you're not satisfied with your current circumstances. Your attitude and expectations impact your life in bigger ways than you can imagine.

246 | Value Your Time

The time is always now.

Alan Watts

You cannot regain any time you've lost. If you don't place enough value on your time, you will always feel that you have very little time. You must spend each moment in time with meaning, purpose, and intention. Then, you can fill your life with treasure.

Develop Keystone Habits | 247

> *Motivation is what gets you started. Habit is what keeps you going.*

Jim Ryun

A keystone habit is a habit that is a side benefit of other changes in your life. Focus on making one change instead of focusing on changing several habits at once. Just like magic, it results in improvements in other areas. Examples of keystone habits are expressing gratitude, getting quality sleep regularly, and guided meditation.

248 | What You Want Now or Most

> *I encourage you to sacrifice what you want now for what you want most.*
>
> *Moustafa Kadous*

Each time you make a choice that leads to instant gratification, it is proof that you have weak motivators. If your reasons "why" are strong enough, there's a low chance that you will make a choice that favors instant gratification.

The best way to accomplish your long-term goals is to ensure that the satisfaction you get from what you want most is always stronger than the satisfaction from what you want now.

The Folly of Loafing Around | 249

> *A hardworking man is better than a crowd of loafers.*

Swedish proverb

Don't be tempted to think people who loaf around have it better. With time, your sacrifice of short-term gains for long-term benefits will shine through, and the loafers will experience the negative consequences of their laziness.

As these loafers start regretting their previous actions and inactions, you will smile when you remember your past sacrifices and be happy that you never gave in to the easy route by loafing around.

250 | Collaboration Makes You Better

> *Competition makes us faster, collaboration makes us better.*
>
> *Nancy Steiger*

When you have the support of others, it becomes easier for you to fight against temptations and stick to your resolutions. Whether it's from a book or a conversation, learning from other people's experience makes things easier as well.

Working with a reputable coach can help you accomplish your goals faster. You should also choose an accountability partner who can push you when you don't feel like doing anything.

Multiplicity of Success | 251

Consistency is the key to success.

Tony Robbins

Success in one area of your life results in success in other areas. If you don't believe in your abilities to succeed, choose a skill that only requires practice and practice until you become good at it.

Once you notice progress – based on your judgment of progress, not others – you will discover that you have the power to tackle other challenges in your life. A side benefit of this strategy is that you will develop proper habits and traits to achieve success in all areas of your life.

252 | No Mistake Is Unimportant

> *Life is a journey, not a destination. Learn to enjoy the ride.*
>
> Ralph Waldo Emerson

If, by your judgment, you consider a mistake is unimportant, you will be tempted to let go and ignore it. However, ignoring this seemingly unimportant mistake sets a precedent for tolerating small errors. This doesn't mean you have to seek perfection. You only have to ensure that you don't take any error or mistakes for granted and learn from them.

Help Others Win | 253

> *Helping others gives you opportunities for more wins. Each time your partner wins, you're also a winner.*

Moustafa Kadous

Since we are wired to compete, we may have the mindset of trying to one-up others. However, true smart achievers help others to win. You must be comfortable with this idea to do it well. The payback is faster results for yourself, too. That's when you will be the best, have the best, and deliver the best results.

254 | Friendship Doesn't Translate into Business Compatibility

> *Friends don't always make the best of business partners.*
>
> *Chris Campbel*

It can be an exciting opportunity to enter a business partnership with a friend. However, don't expect that your relationship will translate into a successful commercial union. Even if you share similar values and philosophies, you may not share the same approach to solving business tasks.

Do you still want to start a business with your friend? Communicate about everything clearly, including each other's job titles and responsibilities right from the beginning. Make sure no matter what happens with the business, your friendship will remain intact.

Adapt to Succeed | 255

> *A failure to adapt is the failure to move forward.*

John Wooden

When there are changes in conditions, don't become one of those who complains about it or uses that change in conditions as an excuse for not taking action, be mindful not to become immobilized by worry. Instead, identify opportunities in these changing conditions and act upon them – this is adaptation.

This ability to adapt successfully in the midst of changing conditions is what makes successful people consistently successful. Learn to become aware of your environment and what's changing in it. Then, adapt accordingly.

256 | Learn to Want Things You Already Have

> *You don't need more time; you only need to be more disciplined with the time available to you.*
>
> *Moustafa Kadous*

I am an addict of intermittent fasting where you alternate between eating and abstaining from food regularly. During this state, you will appreciate the value of what you have compared with what you don't need. For example, a simple apple is more than sufficient as a food source. You don't need apple pancakes with an apple-horseradish sauce.

Your life is already incredible in many aspects. You only need to keep reminding yourself that you can lose this life. It will help you realize the value of what you have.

Make Your Employees Feel Valued | 257

> *If you take care of your employees, they will take care of your customers, and your business will take care of itself.*

J. W. Marriott

I am sure you won't stay very long at a place where your work isn't appreciated enough, and you could be replaced instantly. As a manager who wants his employees to stick around, this isn't the type of environment you want to encourage.

Let your employees know that without them, your company, or your department would be worse off. Make this part of your management routine every day. Share feedback from clients, co-workers, and executives with them.

258 | Hit the Perfect Timing

> *How soon 'not now' becomes 'never'.*
>
> *Martin Luther*

Time flies by pretty quickly. If you miss the proper time to take action, it will be almost impossible for you to restart the activity. But if the timing is wrong, the outcome of the activity will also be wrong. The secret is to find the right context so that you can get the timing right.

Examples of the right context:

- You asked for a raise because you brought a new client to the company, not because your coworker got a raise.
- You started a business or invested after a thorough analysis of the market, including the risks, rewards, and legal aspects, not because you lost your job and decided to become an emergency entrepreneur.

Playing It Safe Can Be Risky | 259

> *Playing it safe is the riskiest choice we can ever make.*

Sarah Ban Breathnach

Risk takers are the most successful people in all walks of life. You need to believe in your ideas, strike out towards your goals, and stand up for what you believe is right. When a situation involves risk and you don't know whether to hold back or go ahead, re-evaluate your goals. What do you want to accomplish? If this risk becomes successful, does it help you towards achieving your goals?

260 | Stay Hungry for More Success

> *Remain hungry, relish your success. But always be ready to do more and achieve more.*
>
> *Moustafa Kadous*

Being successful and staying hungry for success are different concepts. Most people can't maintain their drive for success once they reach a major goal.

From my experience, here are proven ways to stay hungry for success:

- Don't let the success get into your head.
- Make decisions without emotions; think more about what will help you grow.
- Think of success as a journey and not a destination.

The Truth

> *Defeat is not the worst of failures, not to have tried is the true failure.*

George E. Woodberry

A thousand people or more might tell you that today is lousy, but today doesn't have to be lousy for you, too. When people say something can't be done, it doesn't mean that thing is impossible.

Listen to the opinion of others patiently, and think about them carefully. Then, identify the truth, what's working, and what won't work. Always arrive at the truth by doing the work.

262 | Take the Forward Step

> *Leverage your mistakes till you achieve success.*
>
> *Moustafa Kadous*

Don't be like most people who hesitate to work on their goals because of self-doubt or fear of failure.

You must remind yourself that without taking a step forward, you will always remain in the same position. If your forward step was unsuccessful and you need to backtrack, you'll still gain some experience.

You have nothing to lose, but you have a lot to gain.

What goals are you trying to pursue but you are afraid of failing? Consider the fact that your attempt gives you a chance of success, no matter how small, and a 100% learning experience.

Genuine Success | 263

> *Failure is not the opposite of success, it's part of success.*

Arianna Huffington

Create success in your way. Connect the idea of success to your soul and detach it from your ego.

Become aware of the possibilities and abundance around you that will boost your strong desire to make a difference. Take each challenge as an opportunity and transform it into value. Recognize the chance to bring new fulfillment into the world through each person you encounter and in every situation.

Ask yourself, "What can I do today that I will appreciate in the next ten years when I remember today's date?" When you think along this line, you will discover you are aligned toward achieving genuine success.

264 | Success Link

> *Ambition and action are the first and second steps to success.*
>
> *Moustafa Kadous*

The link between thought and action results in success. You won't get anywhere by choosing one and ignoring the other. If you think about what you'll do and how you'll do it, but you don't do it, you won't accomplish anything. Also, if you take hasty actions without putting proper thought into it, you won't achieve anything.

Think, then take action; think more and take more action. Gradually – and with focus – you will be on your way to success...

Don't Settle for Less | 265

The biggest human temptation is to settle for too little.

Thomas Merton

You can benefit from purposeful, focused accomplishments. So, don't settle for less. Will you be filled with gratitude or regret in the future when you think about your current plans? Occupy your time with actions that will add value to your life.

Always remind yourself that there is a better alternative to wasting several minutes or a few hours on meaningless diversions.

266 | Make A Miracle

> *A strong positive mental attitude will create more miracles than any wonder drug.*
>
> *Patricia Neal*

Make someone's life a little less lonely today. Let those around you at this present time experience a fresh form of kindness from you. You have endured an arduous journey to see this day. Use it as an opportunity to love more fully and sincerely than ever before.

Look for dim places where you can shed some light. Make a miracle through your love and push life a little higher.

Don't Be Afraid to Introduce New Ideas | 267

> It's not about ideas. It's about making ideas happen.

Scott Belsky

Unfortunately, people with the boldest ideas are often disregarded. We were taught from an early age to conform to what everyone else does. Though it can be great to fill an existing role, you need to think differently to do things differently.

Don't throw away your idea because it's new or different. Put a plan around it and go for it if it makes sense.

Chapter Ten

FOCUS

Daily tips to bring unshakeable focus that will help you unlock your best self.

> " Everybody says they want to be free. Take the train off the tracks and it's free; but it can't go anywhere."
>
> Zig Ziglar

268 | Work Your Plan Daily

Plan your work for today and every day, then work your plan.

Margaret Thatcher

The more you talk about your intentions, the less action you will take upon them. Stop admiring your plan, and start working it. Since expectations drive results, jump into action now to create the most powerful expectations.

There is plenty of work for you to do. So, stop making excuses, talking, planning, wishing, or waiting.

Little Details Matter

> *Details matter; it's worth waiting to get it right.*
>
> Steve Jobs

Little things can deliver a huge impact. However, you control whether that impact will be positive or negative. Don't let the little things run your life; but learn to master them.

Keep a clear purpose in your mind, and let the small details work in your favor.

270 | Be Specific

> *The palest ink is more reliable than the most powerful memory.*
>
> *Chinese proverb*

Make it a habit to write down your goals. They don't have to be lengthy – one or two sentences will do. Then your goals become real-world resolutions and not just some ideas floating through your head which you can disregard anytime.

Journal the actions your take each day toward the achievement of the big goal. It makes you more accountable to yourself and boosts your motivation to keep going. And, you'll gain more clarity about how close you are to achieving your goal.

Pursue Less with Discipline

> *Success is nothing more than a few simple disciplines, practiced every day.*
>
> *Jim Rohn*

Most people find it difficult to say no. Consequently, they say yes to new obligations and wonder how they've consumed so much energy.

They don't create the time to remove non-essentials from their lives to focus on their priorities. Embrace the strategy of pursuing less, It will help you retain control over your life. Find out what you can eliminate from your life to create room for what matters to you.

Consider eliminating needless routine or common daily tasks with something that ignites your creativity and improves your skills. Finally, think twice before adding new events to your calendar or accepting any new obligations.

272 | Stop Doing Anything You Don't Want to Do

> *When you agree to do what you don't want to do, you will resent the person who asked you to do it.*
>
> *James Altucher*

When next you're tempted to say yes just to prevent an awkward feeling, practice your self-control by saying no. Keep in mind, however that you still need to help those who seek your help; you only need to establish boundaries and stick with them.

A good way to get started with this new habit is to start saying no on little things. For example, offer limited help or attach some conditions when you offer your help. Even if you don't want to refuse completely, exercise your power to determine when you will be available and the kind of help you can offer.

Your Opportunity to Climb Higher | 273

> *Use your life experience as a stepping stone to greater heights.*

Moustafa Kadous

Right now, you have more experience than the previous years of your life; you are at the peak of your experience. Sometimes during this journey, you've enjoyed the good moments and learned to navigate the challenges you've faced. Now, you are at the summit of your life experience.

Your next step is to use all these experiences as an opportunity to climb higher. If you keep going with determination and gratitude, you will experience mountains of more experiences that enrich your life.

274 | Unanswered Questions

> *Live your life; answers to unanswered questions will show up in time.*
>
> — *Moustafa Kadous*

Despite all your best efforts, you'll encounter questions or problems you won't be able to resolve or find a suitable solution. It is rare to resolve all issues before specific deadlines. But the truth is, you can still have a great night's sleep, a delightful weekend, and long life despite these unanswered questions.

Don't put your life on hold because you want to solve all your problems. Work diligently to resolve your issues, but don't let any unresolved issue prevent you from doing well or living well.

Drop Unnecessary Tasks | 275

Success demands singleness of purpose.

Vince Lombardi

You can eliminate the need for complex planning systems by simplifying your to-do list. Get that list down to the barest essentials. A long to-do list can be overwhelming, especially when it doesn't have any prioritization.

Spend a few minutes to review your task and project lists; your goal is to simplify them. Prioritize each item that's essential to the next step. Cross out all unnecessary tasks and delegate tasks that can be to others.

276 | Keep a Laser-Focus

> *The successful warrior is the average man with laser-like focus.*

Bruce Lee

Before you can unlock the best you, you must identify specific areas of your life where you need to improve and how you intend to make such improvements. For example, if you get angry quite easily, focus on improving your self-control. If you find it difficult to wake up early, figure out ways to boost your self-discipline in the mornings.

Here's how to tackle both these issues. When you're angry and before you vent, take a few moments to collect your thoughts. Also, use "I" statements to describe the problem without being disrespectful. For example, "I'm upset because you didn't offer to help with the dishes before leaving the table" is a better statement than "you never do any house chores."

If you find it difficult to wake up early, figure out ways to boost your self-discipline in the mornings.

Plan to do something you love when you first wake up. When you're excited about your early morning plan, you'll see the snooze button as a distraction.

With a laser-focus, you will become more effective at strengthening your willpower muscle.

277 | Don't Choose Bitterness

> *Choose to be better, not bitter.*
>
> — *Moustafa Kadous*

Unless you choose to be bitter, nothing can make you bitter – not people, situations, or even twists of fate. Bitterness doesn't add any value to your life whether you let it last for a day or a lifetime.

A simple and effective way to avoid being affected by the bitterness is to get past it quickly. Learn the lessons from the source of your bitterness to make you better, and get on with life. Don't let any bitterness, no matter how small, hold you back. You still have a lot of good to live for and to do.

Drop Your Electronics Addiction | 278

If you can quit for a day, you can quit for a lifetime.

Benjamin Alire Saenz

With modern technology, you can accomplish a whole lot – connect with your loved ones or people all over the world, learn, and make money. In simple terms, technology is a blessing, but it can also become an addiction.

As with excess in anything, too much technology is the problem and not the technology itself. So periodically, go on short technology fasts and check your phone less often than usual.

279 | Quit Pretending

> *Be careful when you pretend to be someone else, you might forget your true self.*
>
> *Moustafa Kadous*

The conflict you have with yourself is the easiest conflict to avoid, but it's also one of the most painful types of conflicts. You experience energy drain, and your credibility is damaged when the person inside of you conflicts with the person you are on the outside.

An instant way to eliminate this conflict is to be completely honest about yourself. Quit pretending, and you'll free yourself from a heavy burden. Allow your true personality to show forth so that you can fulfill your unique wonderful possibilities.

Be Assertive When You Need To | 280

> *Assertiveness is not what you do, it's who you are!*

Shakti Gawain

The best way to deliver your message successfully is to be assertive. If you're too passive or too aggressive in your communication, people will only react to your delivery and not your message. Behaving assertively improves your self-confidence, self-esteem, and decision-making skills.

Practicing saying no, especially when you face a lot of requests, is one way to be assertive. Instead of accepting the requests and being overwhelmed by them, try saying, "I'm sorry, I can't do that for now." Don't offer any explanation.

281 | Understand the Importance of Self-Refusal

> *You can't get rid of a part that makes you you and be happy.*
>
> *Ingrid Law*

It is neither easy nor fun to deny yourself nice things. But it can be a powerful way to test your character and discover more about yourself.

Self-refusal gives you the chance to understand your true necessities. Until you stay away from your needs, you won't discover the ones that you truly need versus the ones that you think you need.

Self-refusal acts as an emergency brake that stops you from spiraling into overindulgence.

Get started today. Deny yourself of your needs for one day and uncover the ones that are true needs.

Embrace the Philosophy of Subtraction | 282

> *Start making subtractions in your life the moment you notice that the additions have become a burden.*

Moustafa Kadous

If you feel like you have no control over your life or are overburdened, then it's time to change your life philosophy from the addition philosophy to the subtraction philosophy.

Subtraction philosophy involves thinking twice before accepting any new responsibilities, feeling proud of having leisure time, and even simplifying your life and freeing up your calendar.

Subtraction might also involve removing bad habits, negative thoughts, and people who have a negative or bad influence on you.

List all the things in life that are most important to you. Then, remove those things that don't matter.

283 | Restrain from Hasty and Unfocused Behaviors

> Working slowly in today's world goes against every thought system. You can only work slowly by doing it deliberately. Being deliberate requires you to stay in the process, to work in the present moment.

Thomas Sterner

It takes a lot of self-control to work deliberately especially when the stakes are high. When stress threatens to consume you, maintain your focus, and resist the temptation to rush things.

Consciously identify your hasty and unfocused behaviors. Then, use such opportunities to exercise your willpower; do things slowly and precisely.

Focus More on Your Important Gains | 284

> Essentialists see trade-offs as an inherent part of life, not as an inherently negative part of life. Rather than ask, "What do I have to give up, they ask, "What do I want to go big on?

Greg McKeown

Always think about giving up a harmful behavior not as a form of sacrifice, but as an act of empowerment. For example, when you want to improve your peace of mind, treat your family to a nice vacation, and spend less time shopping.

Make sure you understand deep down within you that it is not an act of sacrificing one thing to get something else; it's an act of choosing something you consider more important.

285 | Develop Self-Discipline

> *Discipline is the bridge between goals and accomplishments.*
>
> Jim Rohn

The skill of self-discipline is one of the most important life skills you need to develop. Without self-discipline, you will be easily overwhelmed, have financial problems, be distracted, and a whole lot more.

Taking small actions, things so small you simply can't say no, is one of the first steps to getting better at self-discipline. For starters, find just five things to declutter or run for ten minutes.

Use Your Ten Minutes Well | 286

> *Wasted time is worse than wasted money.*

Paulo Coelho

If most of your free time comes in short blocks, then it is highly likely that you're wasting all this free time. You may be staring at the computer aimlessly or wondering how on earth that the minutes slipped quickly by without notice and without being used for any valuable task.

So, why not develop a list of ten-minute tasks? Then, when you have your ten-minute blocks of free time, you can run down this list and do one or two of them.

287 | Time Wasted Can Never Be Regained

> *A man who dares to waste an hour has not discovered the value of life.*

Charles Darwin

While timekeeping can be an excellent organizational tool, it can also be the biggest way to waste your life. Set in motion now whatever you need to do, want to do, or aspire to do.

When you want to do something, don't leave it unfinished or halfway; go all in. Use the time you have to boss up everything you do; there is no time to mess with your life.

Rank and Responsibility | 288

Rank does not confer privilege or give power. It imposes responsibility.

Peter Drucker

The current global economy is creating more opportunities and more hazards for everyone.

It is now compulsory for companies to make wholesome changes to compete, prosper, and even survive.

Once you become a person of authority, at work or any other place, you must care for and drive accountability among your people.

289 | A Calm Mind in the Face of Challenge

> *Your calm mind is the ultimate weapon against your challenges. So, relax.*
>
> *Bryant McGill*

When all your thoughts seem negative and there are problems everywhere you face, take a break to clear away your thoughts. Then, allow the feeling of serenity to fill your head. Use your resources and abilities to come up with a well-considered, calmly executed response. Any emotional onslaught will only intensify the problem. Rise above the impulse of your ego, it will push you to panic.

During tough times, it is normal to question your self-worth. Consequently, you shouldn't make any decisions during those times. Practice techniques such as mindfulness to calm your anxious mind; it will relieve you of all negative, overcrowding thoughts. Then, you can make your decision.

Sharpen Your Focus | 290

> *Don't lose your focus on your big goals; they will become reality soon.*

Moustafa Kadous

The moment you switch your mindset to "being in it for the long haul," things will start falling into place. Instead of trying to learn how to play the piano in one month, which is not particularly realistic, you will have a better chance to master the piano by developing a routine. For example, practice ten minutes a day six days per week and with consistency for the next six to seven months.

Apply this technique to other areas of your life. Analyze your goals and your approach to those goals. You need self-discipline to maintain a long-term focus in all your endeavors. Replace short-term actions with those that reinforce the commitment that you're in it for the long haul.

291 | Self-Discipline Is Freedom

> *Through discipline comes freedom.*
>
> *Aristotle*

You become more self-disciplined by changing your perception of self-discipline. If your view of self-discipline is deprivation and suffering, you will never enjoy personal growth and will soon give up.

Begin today to view self-discipline as freedom so you will embrace opportunities to practice your self-control.

Simplicity Can Be Profitable | 292

It's simple until you make it complicated; keep it simple.

Jason Fried

The more complicated something appears to be, the less inclined you may be to get started. The truth is that most things aren't as complicated as you imagine them. You only need to educate yourself on the basics and draw your conclusions.

Live by a simple set of rules that give you the freedom to enjoy your life.

293 | Disciplined Choices for Character Improvement

> *Discipline is choosing what you want now and what you want most.*
>
> Abraham Lincoln

Though it might take a while for a complete overhaul of your character, you can make several little decisions and embrace specific thought patterns that can influence the change faster. For example, you may not desire some foods when you start a new diet routine. But if you persist long enough, the desire will build by itself.

Regardless of the area where you want to make a change, what seems like an act of deprivation or sacrifice now can become an important part of your life with time.

Focus on Your Purpose | 294

Believe the plan; don't lose focus.

Moustafa Kadous

There will always be distractions that will keep you from staying focused. The only way to get rid of those distractions is to make the object of your focus hugely important. Your focus becomes stronger when you can connect what you are doing with your biggest reason for doing it.

If you feel your focus is starting to wane, reaffirm, and reconnect to your purpose. You will keep acting with powerful focus as long as you live with an authentic purpose. Focus each moment and each action your dream till your dreams become a reality.

295 | Use the Power of Deadlines

> *A dream is just a dream. A goal is a dream with a plan and a deadline.*
>
> *Harvey MacKay*

Without dreams, you will only be wandering through life, and you can't realize or achieve your dreams without a plan.

Start a vision board. The first step to achieving anything you want in life is to write down your dreams with a concrete goal and include a deadline.

Keep in mind that the dreams on your vision board are not set in stone. They should be solid goals you intend to accomplish when the deadlines you have set for yourself draw closer. Adjust your plan as needed to keep your dreams alive.

Pay Attention to What's Around You | 296

> *Make every detail perfect, and limit the number of details to perfect.*

Jack Dorsey

Slow down and pay attention to what's around you one day, and take a break from your usual routine of thinking about your destination. Walk to work on one of your workdays. If that's not possible, walk to the grocery store.

You will be surprised at what you'll notice. You'll spot routes you've never seen before, hear birds and smell plants that may open a whole new experience for you.

297 | Focus on Deep Work, Not Shallow Work

> *First, identify and then complete your most important tasks.*
>
> *Moustafa Kadous*

Shallow work is what you do to avoid real work, and that never gets you closer to your goals. Deep work focuses on getting the most important tasks done that also have the highest impact.

There is a big difference between being busy, which shallow work can accomplish, and being efficient or effective.

Work more efficiently. Separate your important tasks from urgent ones. Then, complete these important tasks when you have your optimal energy levels.

Gain Clarity | 298

> *Clarity affords focus.*

Thomas Leonard

The main ingredients of one's mental makeup are confusion, distraction, and disorganization.
- Confusion shows up as unclear priorities since your future path isn't clear or decisive.
- Distraction shows up as several little things that pull your attention in other, perhaps useless directions.
- Disorganization shows up as unorderly thoughts that inhibit productivity.

Here's how you can gain clarity on these ingredients:
- Confusion – get your priorities straight.
- Distraction – improve your power of focus.
- Disorganization – take care of important things first.

Record all your tasks, thoughts, questions, and ideas in Evernote or any other productivity app. Come back to sort them later, just be sure to capture them in the moment.

299 | Choose Your Highest Priorities

> *Action expresses priorities*
>
> *Mohandas Gandhi*

Having a vision of your ideal future will help you identify the priorities that can help you achieve your goals.

Use the steps below to choose your highest priorities.

- Write down things you wish you could do regularly as an appendix to the list of what you currently do regularly,
- Group these tasks into categories. For example, the wellness category can contain exercises and daily meditation.
- Choose three categories that can impact your life positively for the next six months.
- Print them and put them in an obvious place where you can always see them

Limit Your Time for Specific Tasks | 300

> *You don't need more time in your day. You need to decide.*

Seth Godin

When you set a time limit to complete certain tasks, it makes you more productive and makes it almost impossible to procrastinate. For example, if you are putting off a task because it is unpleasant, do it now. But, allot only 40% of the time to get it done than is your usual pattern.

The excitement and challenge of completing it in a shorter timeframe should fuel your resolve to complete it.

301 | Early Morning

> *One small productive activity in the morning is a blessing for the remainder of the day.*

Moustafa Kadous

For most people, including me, early mornings are free of distractions. It is no wonder that most successful people wake up early. Exercising is one of the best ways to start your day. It helps you set the tone for the day - a conscious decision to take action based on self-control and dedication.

Start including exercise in your morning routine. It doesn't have to be an entire workout. It can be a quick walk around the block, some stretching, or a few reps of some simple exercises.

Life's Humility | 302

> *A negative mind will never give you a positive life.*

Ziad K. Abdelnour

Humility improves your effectiveness, your experiences, and your connection with what's important in life. Always be open about what you do not know; it will increase the depth of your knowledge.

Express gratitude for the humbling experience of your plans that go awry. When life humbles, emerge from the experience stronger than ever.

303 | Expand What Works

> *Remember, what you focus on expands; results follow focus.*
>
> — *Marcus Buckingham*

You can't destroy what's right to change what's wrong. just as you can't cut down those who prosper as a means to lift those who suffer.

Build on what works to change what doesn't work. Expand on existing success to create new, more widespread success. You do this by identifying what improves your life – your treasures and value – and focusing on doing more of that.

Move Past Distractions | 304

Starve your distractions; feed your focus.

Imam Ali

The assault from distractions never stops, but you have the ability, will, and strength to live beyond it all. Become aware of what's most important to you and you can power past your distractions.

Know yourself, your passions, and what you care about the most. Distractions won't distract you for long once you can feed your purpose into the power intention.

305 | In Peace

> *Until you make peace with who you are, you'll never be content with what you have.*
>
> *Doris Mortman*

Peace improves your focus and effectiveness by giving you great positive power. Stop assuming that you need to fight before you can prevail. Allow the power of peace to lift you higher than any conflict.

Allow peace to settle into your day. Replace thoughts that push peace away – conflict, judgment, revenge, retribution, and separateness – with those that attract peace – forgiveness and understanding.

Look with Objectivity | 306

> *Dispassionate objectivity is itself a passion for the real and the truth.*

Abraham Maslow

A way to look at your situation with objectivity is to refuse to make the situation about you. For example, assuming your problem happened to someone else, what advice would you give to that person?

Focus on an effective response to a difficult situation and detach yourself from emotional burdens and biases. Imagine yourself to be a disciplined and successful person. With that perspective, how would you handle the situation?

When you open yourself to a wider spectrum of possibilities, you will discover that you are powerful and more effective than you think.

307 | Focus on Positive Thoughts Even When Feeling Negative

> *Being positive doesn't mean ignoring the negative. Being positive means overcoming the negative.*
>
> *Marcandangel*

Take the steps to make positive thinking your second nature. Always project confidence that you can break out from the negative cycle regardless of your current situation.

Spend time every day to read positive and inspirational materials that encourage positive thoughts, like the *Holy Book, Unlock the Best You*, and spiritual passages. It is a great way to start and end your day since you can focus on what's important to you in life.

Minimize Your Needs | 308

> *A man is rich in proportion to the number of things he can afford to let go.*

Henry David Thoreau

If you can accomplish your goals without the right resources, then you are stronger and more capable than the person who can't do so. However, this doesn't mean that you should deliberately reject the resources available to you.

Look at the lack of resources more as an encouragement that you can still make it big despite not having the best tools available to you. Apply this approach to other areas of your life: learn a new skill yourself without a coach or a teacher.

309 | Say What You Want

> *A clear goal and purpose are the secret to a great day.*
>
> — *Moustafa Kadous*

You must say what you want clearly and specifically before you can get it. Whether it's from yourself or someone else, ask specifically, and you'll receive specifically.

If you are struggling to know the right steps that will lead to accomplishing your goals, then you need to articulate your goals in a specific and more compelling way. Why? You will have a specific goal which differs from a wish, a vague idea of something nice.

Chapter Eleven

HONESTY & DREAMS FOR THE FUTURE

Actionable tips to be honest with yourself as you bring your dream future to reality.

> "With integrity you have nothing to fear, since you have nothing to hide. With integrity you will do the right thing, so you will have no guilt. With fear and guilt removed, you are free to be and do your best."
>
> Zig Ziglar

310 | Create Your Circumstances

> *Man is not the creature of circumstances;*
> *circumstances are the creatures of men.*
>
> Benjamin Disraeli

Wouldn't it be nice to hold someone else accountable for what happens in our lives? Fortunately, or unfortunately, we create our own realities. Acknowledge that you always have control over your circumstances rather than just accept your circumstances and do nothing. It's your choice. You can change, accept, or find power in your circumstances.

If you don't like your current environment, move to another place. If you really can't move to a different place, focus on the positive aspects of living where you are. Seek out some hidden benefits of living in that environment. For example, a big town might not be great for the cost of living, but job prospects can be great. Create a better future for yourself by creating your circumstances.

New Day, New Life

> *Don't let the disappointments of the past steal today's peace or kill tomorrow's joy.*

Moustafa Kadous

The past cannot come back again; it is gone forever. Today, you are willing, determined, and purposeful. Make real and lasting progress with this new day. You can do whatever you desire to do.

Starting from today, create your life to be the best you've always imagined it could be. There are unlimited possibilities in this day. Use them as your energy and motivation that inspires you to take action. Right now, allow life to encourage you, support you, and pull you to your best.

312 | Dream, Believe, Achieve

> If you don't build your dream, someone will hire you to help build theirs.

Tony A. Gaskins Jr.

Dream

Your dreams begin by imagining what you want to achieve. Sit down with a blank sheet of paper. Think forward and write down your dreams, emphasizing why they are important to you and what you can do to reach them.

Believe

You need a "high enough" level of self-esteem. When you need an extra boost, find inspiration from others who have overcome bigger obstacles than you. Believe that you will achieve your dreams with time.

Achieve

Once believed, you can only achieve your dreams by setting concrete goals to get there. Break down your goals by quarter, month, week, day, and even by the hour. Create a vision board, a physical representation of your goals. Need inspiration? Search Google!

Your Past Doesn't Define Your Future

> *Every sinner has a future, and every saint has a past.*

Oscar Wilde

No matter how good you are at anything, you have failed at some point, in some way. Yet, you are not so bad that you cannot change for the better. Regardless of your past failures, you have an opportunity to be a better person.

Focus on thinking about your legacy and how you would want people to describe your character when asked. Once you've settled on that future perception, start acting that way every day, every time, and everywhere.

314 | Dreams Come True

> *Dreams come true; without that possibility, nature would not incite us to have them.*
>
> *John Updike*

No matter your dream, you can accomplish it. One proven way to make your dream come true is to strip down your goals. You will have a clear evaluation of what you truly want when you peel back layers surrounding your objective. Also, you must be specific about your dream. It will be easier to chart the path to get there.

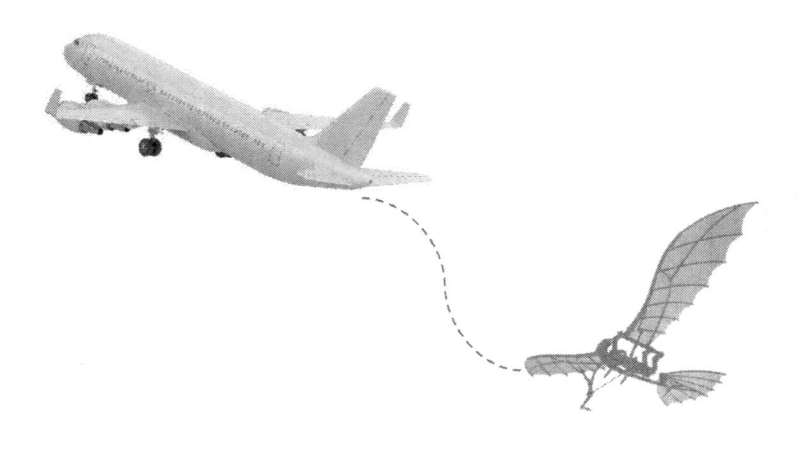

In Pursuit of Dreams

> *Happiness is not a station you arrive at, but a manner of traveling.*

Margaret Lee Runbeck

Stop believing that more money or accomplishing your goals is the only thing that will bring you happiness. If you continue holding onto that belief, then you are cultivating a habit that your happiness depends on the circumstances of your life. Sadly, these circumstances can be taken away at any moment, and poof, your happiness goes away immediately. Taking stock of your blessings and expressing sincere gratitude for them is the best way to find happiness in your life.

From today, start expressing gratitude for the good things in your life, and you will cultivate true happiness even as you work towards achieving your goals.

316 | Small Promises Count

> *Breaking little promises is proof that you'll break the big ones as well.*

Moustafa Kadous

Small promises and big promises are equally important. Holding someone's trust in you and keeping their confidence is a big relationship promise. Repaying loans is a big financial promise. Calling someone when you say you will, is another promise. While you might take the big ones more seriously, don't dismiss the small promises.

Build trust and your reputation by taking the minor promises seriously. The side benefit of keeping these small promises is that you show that you are also organized and responsible.

Great Hope

Let your hopes, not your hurts, shape your future.

Robert H. Schuller

Since you have great hope for today, nothing can stop you from acting on that hope. You may not realize all your hopes, but it is better to live with hope than live without it.

Though you don't know what your future holds, you can only hope for a better future. Put that hope into action by positively directing your thoughts, actions, time, and life.

318 | Into the Future

> See things in the present, even if they are in the future.
>
> *Larry Ellison*

While you can bring your past experiences and values into your future, you can't bring the past itself. In this ever-changing world, you cannot return to the past or remain stagnant. You can do better than what you currently think, feel, or do. Be ready to move forward into the future tirelessly. Then, you can create a bright and fulfilling future.

Enable the Future

Your task is to enable the future, not foresee it

Antoine de Saint Exupery

Here's a little exercise for you....
Focus on one part of your ideal future. Let's choose your finances. It is highly likely that you want more money, afford anything you desire, and never have money worries again.

Now back to the present. Ask yourself, "Am I enabling or disabling my desired future through my past and present choices?"

If you always consider the future before making your decisions, you'll learn to make better decisions today. Consequently, you will improve your effectiveness, discipline, and experience fulfillment today. Make choices that help you to live well today and create your best future.

320 | Be Willing to Be Imperfect.

A great man is always willing to be little.

Ralph Waldo Emerson

If you can never see yourself as small, humility and modesty would be impossible aims for you.

Humility helps prevent you from swinging between confidence and over-confidence. It allows you to realize that the more you know, the more you need to learn.

Accept that you are imperfect and stop toying with your ego by analyzing whether you are inferior or superior to others. You are neither.

Honor and Integrity, Always | 321

Be fair to others, speak with credibility, and keep your promise.

Moustafa Kadous

The way you view yourself is the real benefit of being honorable; it's not to win the admiration of others. As you journey through life, treat these traits as guideposts to live with honor and integrity.

- Deal with others in fairness and with honor.
- Stand for honesty and speak with credibility.
- Keep your promise; it is as important to the recipient as it is to you.

322 | Listen to Your Gut

> *Trust your hunches; they're usually based on facts filed away just below the conscious level.*
>
> — *Dr. Joyce Brothers*

Instead of using a rational thinking process to make your decision, sometimes it's better to listen to your gut. Gut feelings are there for a reason, and its usually right most times. Don't ignore them.

The next time you want to make a decision, when deep down you no longer care about your goal or it now makes you feel uneasy, let your intuition make its case.

Seek Genuine Friendships Not Convenient Ones

> *Genuine friendship is life.*
>
> Stephanie Lahart

Good friends have a huge positive impact on your happiness and mental health. One way to find true friendship is to focus on the feelings of that friendship and not what it looks like.

Answer the following questions in all honesty:

- Do I feel emotionally free when I am in the company of this person?
- Does this person support and treat me with respect?
- From the few times we've met, can I trust this person?

A good friend will not disregard your needs or require you to compromise your values.

324 | No Matter What, Right Is Right

> *Wrong is wrong even if everyone is doing it; right is right even if no one is doing it.*

Augustine of Hippo

Saying that your negative habits aren't that negative because lots of people engage in it won't make them right.

Stop comparing yourself with the majority. What you should do is to compare yourself with your mentors, even if they are a speck in a crowd.

> DO SOMETHING TODAY THAT YOUR FUTURE SELF WILL THANK YOU FOR

Live Your Beliefs | 325

> *Seek to experience your beliefs and live the life of your dreams.*

Moustafa Kadous

Though it is good to believe the truth, it is even better to experience it for yourself. When you experience the essence of truth, it will establish your knowledge about the truth.

A way to experience your beliefs is to practice them. Seek to experience what you've been told and what you've come to believe. When the truth comes to life in you, it rises to a whole new level.

326 | Tell the Truth, Always

> *Being entirely honest with oneself is a good exercise.*
>
> Sigmund Freud

Regardless of where you go or what you do, there will always be opportunities and temptations for you to lie. But promise yourself that you will always tell the truth regardless of the circumstances.

A simple way to remain honest each time someone asks you a question you'd normally answer with a lie, tell them, "I don't feel like answering that question," and don't give any justifications. You have a right not to explain your decisions.

Keep Promises to Yourself | 327

> *You've made a promise to yourself. Now, keep your promise.*

Moustafa Kadous

We make promises to others all the time, and we feel guilty when we break them. But we are quick to let go of promises we make to ourselves. One reason we break those self-promises is that it is too easy to break them; no one knows about it except you.

Here are proven ways to keep promises to yourself:

- Pretend that the promise is for someone else.
- Write down your promises; they will become visible and increase your chances of following through.

328 | Create Your Ideal Future

> *The best way to predict the future is to invent it.*
>
> *Alan Kay*

Write down what you want in your future on a sheet of paper or in a notebook. Include what you want next year, in the next five years, ten years and even twenty years from now. Examples of what should be on your list could include:

- supporting a comfortable lifestyle without debts.
- doing consulting and coaching work for interest purposes instead of financial benefit.
- enjoying a happy married life.

Then, integrate items from the list of your ideal future into your present day.

Speak with Integrity

> *Be impeccable with your word. Speak with integrity. Say only what you mean. Use the power of your word in the direction of truth and love towards yourself.*

Miguel Angel Ruiz

See where you stand by taking a closer look at how your words and deeds connect, or don't. Integrity boosts personal power significantly and this power reduces each time you undermine your integrity through your words or actions.

Make careful use of your language, and when you agree to things, show up for your agreements.

Develop a greater awareness of how you use your words, and stop making disempowering statements about yourself. When your words aren't positive, change them.

Chapter Twelve

SELF-CARE & SELF-DEVELOPMENT

Daily tips to take care of your physical, emotional, and spiritual self.

> "When I discipline myself to eat properly, live morally, exercise regularly, grow mentally and spiritually. And not put any drugs or alcohol, I have given myself the freedom to be at my best, perform at my best, and reap all the rewards that go along with it."
>
> Zig Ziglar

330 | Ignore the World When You're Down

> "You may see me struggle, but you will never see me quit."
>
> *Tom Coleman*

Few people lend a helping hand or offer words of support when you are down. But when you become successful, everyone will confess that they've known you for a long time.

During your struggle periods, stay far away from bad energy. Get up, work, and keep going until you accomplish your dreams. Also, reward those who were with you with gratitude while you were struggling.

Respect and Appreciate Your Body | 331

Respect and love yourself first. Others will love you with trust.

Debasish Mridha

Exercising shouldn't be about building a perfect body; it should be about respecting and appreciating your body. Once healthy living becomes a habit, in the same way you care for your prized possessions, you can set the fitness goals that strengthen your body further. Now, your only goal is for your actions to show respect toward your body.

332 | Make Physical Exercise a Habit

> *I hated every minute of training, but I said, 'don't quit.' Suffer now and live the rest of your life as a champion.*
>
> *Muhammad Ali*

There is more to an active lifestyle than physical fitness or a stoic work ethic. Which of these options would you prefer?

a. A fun physical activity for seven days a week, thirty minutes each time?

b. Sixty minutes of joyless exercise five days a week?

The answer is obvious; option "a" provides fun and enjoyment which are vital rewards; these rewards result in the formation of habits.

Appreciate Your Relationships, Self, Life, and Others | 333

> *Feeling gratitude and not expressing it is like wrapping a present and not giving it.*

William Arthur Ward

You'll gain several benefits when you appreciate yourself, appreciate your relationships, appreciate life and others. When you appreciate what you have right now, you will appreciate what you had all along.

Two ways to start practicing appreciation is journaling and sharing your gratitude with others. Through journaling, you'll establish a daily practice where you remind yourself of the good things, benefits, graces, and gifts that you enjoy. You'll also strengthen your relationships by expressing gratitude to those who did appreciable things for you. Smiling, saying thank you, and writing letters of gratitude are actions that can trigger emotions of appreciation. So, use them often.

334 | Engage, Evolve, and Elevate

> *When you engage, you evolve, and when you evolve, you elevate.*
>
> Moustafa Kadous

ENGAGE
Engagement helps you to find or retain the passion for your beliefs and daily life; increasing your engagement level boosts your productivity. You need to see value or purpose in your pursuits to prevent decreasing levels of engagement. It may help to speak with a personal or business coach to discover the best environment that suits your interests and keeps you engaged.

EVOLVE
Oftentimes, your struggles, difficulties, and obstacles are the universes' way of forcing you to change. Your first step is to ask yourself, "How have I evolved?" Compare how you handled a friend hurting your feelings during elementary school to how you handle the same issue now that you are an adult. Learn to use these situations, including criticism and feedback, to learn, grow, and evolve in whatever you do. You can only make a positive

change when you understand how your soul, mind, and body operate as one.

ELEVATE

One purpose of your soul in the physical world is to elevate self-awareness of your thoughts and emotions. Few people realize or understand this beautiful way to live their lives. Raising your self-awareness allows you to have a different perspective about life, people, and situations. While it is a process that takes time, practicing meditation, intention, and introspection areas across all areas of your life helps you move toward achieving joy, balance, and harmony in your life.

335 | Monitor Yourself Carefully and Frequently

> When you monitor yourself with more care and frequency, you'll have better control of yourself.
>
> *Roy Baumeister*

Self-monitoring is an important tool to track your results, stick with your goals, and achieve your goals.

If you can't monitor yourself daily, make sure you include it as part of your weekly schedule. For example, weighing yourself daily and regularly monitoring your physique in the mirror helps you to keep yourself in check even when you are already fit.

Live for Yourself | 336

The rest of my life is going to be my best life.

Moustafa Kadous

Make your life as amazing as you desire it; you're in control of your life. Want a break from dating? Do so. Want to spend a day reading in bed? Do it, and enjoy it. Do things because you want to, not because someone tells you to do it.

Fill your life with joy every day so that when you reflect on it, you will realize the fabulousness of doing so.

337 | Surprise Your Body

> *Your body is a strong machine, but you have to fuel it with a powerful mind.*
>
> *Gymaholic*

Boring workouts are one common reason why people don't succeed in making permanent exercise a habit in their lives. After a doing the same routine a few times, the body adapts that routine and stops responding the same way it did at the beginning.

What you need to do is to mix up your exercise routines from time to time. Focus on different aspects of the exercise; change the place where you exercise; change your exercise partners, or add one. As a result, you can boost your excitement, surprise your body, and stick with the physical activity for the long term.

Suggestions from Buddha | 338

> *The best way to take care of the future is to take care of the present moment.*

Thich Nhat Hanh

You will have more effective communication by getting into the business at hand quickly. While you can initiate a conversation through small talk, do not engage in lazy conversations, such as complaints, criticism of others, or gossip. However,

Don't oversleep. It is a scientifically proven fact that oversleeping doesn't deliver any benefits. You only need to sleep more when you need to recover from an illness or a difficult workout.

Do not chase after desires. Focus on important things and not your temporary urges.

339 | Fresh Understanding

> *The key to all of life is understanding how to add value to others.*

Jay Abraham

You need commitment, patience, time, humility, and mental effort to gain understanding. Despite the effort it can take, understanding others creates useful options for you. For example, you can cooperate with someone else for a mutual benefit once you understand that person's perspective.

Seek fresh understanding through learning and adding value to others. Then, work towards it.

For each fresh understanding, you open the door to more understanding and enrich what you already understand.

Observe Your Emotions and Seek a Different Exit | 340

> *Regardless of the emotions building up within you, always be honest with yourself about your feelings.*

Nigel Cumberland

Don't pretend to yourself that you don't feel your temptations; it won't make those urges disappear.

A better option is to observe your emotions and seek a different exit. Sometimes, the temptation to take it easy is your body's cry for help to stop overworking yourself.

For example, you might prevent an unplanned cheat week in your diet by scheduling a cheat meal to indulge yourself a little.

341 | Avoid Temptations

> *Temptation is a ... man's excuse.*
>
> — H. L. Mencken

Suppose you are looking online for information that can grow your business, but you encounter a funny video accidentally. You can choose to continue with your search or watch the funny video. While you can blame external factors for your slip up by watching the funny video, it is not a legitimate excuse.

Your best option is to remove all distractions from your environment. From the example above, using a website blocker such as freedom can be your best solution for removing all forms of distraction.

Pain and Quitting | 342

> *The regret of doing nothing when you ought to do something is more painful than the pain from growth or change.*

Moustafa Kadous

The desire to avoid pain and the desire to have pleasure are two very powerful motivators, but the former is stronger than the latter. If you're yet to do something which you are supposed to have done, it is highly likely that there's some pain associated with it. Though taking action will lead to your pleasure, your desire to avoid pain is preventing you from doing what you need to do.

A simple and effective solution is to focus on the pain of not doing it – the bigger, long-term pain. You'll feel more motivated to take action. It can be painful to learn a new skill or do anything that will improve your life. But when you consider the long-term pain, it is more painful not to do them.

343 | Use Criticism as Opportunities

> If you are not criticized, you may not be doing much.
>
> *Donald Rumsfeld*

Even world-class top performers fall victim to criticisms. Unfortunately, most of us don't appreciate lots of people who've expressed their love for us or our work; rather, we dwell on one occurrence of hatred and allow it to ruin their lives.

But by disregarding hate, you will improve your willpower and self-control. More importantly, you will disengage from negative emotions that can ruin your mood. Take criticisms as positive and constructive feedback and disregard the negative emotions.

Make Walking Regularly a Habit | 344

All truly great thoughts are conceived while walking.

Friedrich Nietzche

Apart from being a fantastic exercise, walking awakens your creativity and boosts your problem-solving skills. Even if it's just for fifteen minutes, make it a habit to walk regularly. For optimal results, choose a route that consists more of natural surroundings or away from the hustle and bustle of city life.

345 | Improve Your Self-Worth

> *You are not your mistakes; they are what you did, not who you are.*
>
> Lisa Lieberman-Wang

Self-awareness is the first step to improving your self-worth. You will need to unlearn some of your childhood thoughts and beliefs as you seek self-awareness.

Some helpful questions that can help you improve your self-awareness are:

- How do visualize your ideal 'you'?
- What are your dreams and goals?
- What do you see as hindrances to achieving these goals or dreams?

A Masquerade of Laziness | 346

> There is nothing more frightful than ignorance in action.

Johann Wolfgang Von Goethe

Ignorance is a manifestation of laziness. It involves bypassing the opportunity to educate yourself willfully. Consequently, it leads to negligence. You must choose to be prepared; don't be ignorant. It is better to know too much than to know too little.

Expand your knowledge constantly to unlock the best you. Even when truth and knowledge lead to difficult questions or are uncomfortable, don't discontinue your self-education. Keep seeking knowledge.

347 | Find a Good Private Teacher

> To excel at the highest level - or any level - you need to believe in yourself, and hands down, one of the biggest contributors to my self-confidence has been private coaching.

Stephen Curry

A sure-fire way to get a positive return quickly is to expand your knowledge and experience in one-on-one coaching. A private coach can fast-track your start to a new change. Most likely, you only have to pay for the initial help. It will be enough for you to get started and keep practicing your knowledge until you accomplish your desired change.

Create a Desire That Drives Learning | 348

...study without desire spoils the memory; it retains nothing that it takes in.

Leonardo da Vinci

The human brain is picky about it what it remembers. So, you'll retain little of what you learn unless you have a good reason to learn it.

If you need to learn about something and you are struggling with it, find an interesting angle about it.

If you can't find any interesting angle about what you want to learn, consider the rewards it offers you and use those rewards as your motivation. Note that the reward doesn't have to be extrinsic, such as a promotion at work. But it must have intrinsic value, such as the challenge it poses and how you are trying to overcome it.

349 | Recognize and Change Bad Beliefs or Habits

> *Your beliefs become your thoughts, your thoughts become your words, your words become your actions, your actions become your habits, your habits become your values, your values become your destiny.*
>
> — *Gandhi*

Your first opportunity to change is when you recognize that your bad habits and beliefs are your enemies. Once you have identified them, you can overcome them by:

- Speak positively about yourself. With time, you will believe your positive affirmations. Once you have accomplished success, write down those affirmations. They will serve as encouragement to push yourself and achieve more when you need an extra boost.
- Consult a coach, especially when your beliefs trigger anxiety, depression, or other similar conditions. A coach has the resources, tools, and knowledge you'll need to overcome challenges and live a more fulfilled life.

Know that there are costs to your bad habits and beliefs. These costs will remain until you make changes in your life.

Infuse Fun into Your Routines | 350

> *A business has to be involving; it has to be fun, and it has to exercise your creative instincts.*

Richard Branson

If you infuse fun and adventure into your daily routine, it will be pleasurable and easier and for you to stick with it. For example, turn your desire to become more financially disciplined into a game. Challenge yourself to save as much as possible. Find better deals for your regular purchases.

If there are opportunities for adventure and entertainment in your daily routine, take them. You'll have higher chances of sticking with them over more boring obligations.

351 | Accelerate Change

> *The secret of change is to focus all your energy not on fighting the old, but on building the new.*

Dan Millman

When you refuse change, resist it, or adapt too slowly to it, you will be increasingly dissatisfied. Your performances will suffer, and you'll experience negative outcomes.

Learning to accelerate the pace of change is one of the important life skills, you must want to accelerate that pace. Learn new ways of working, new concepts, and new ideas and do it now and pick up the pace.

Don't Be Afraid to Grow Slowly | 352

> *Be not afraid of growing slowly, be afraid only of standing still.*

Chinese Proverb

In a world where most people want instant results, I want to remind you that it's okay to grow slowly. No matter how slowly you think you are going, keep making progress. Stay patient and seek long-term solutions; it will boost your character and values.

Show gratitude for your current progress and encourage others on their growth journey.

353 | Be Punctual

> *Through a determination to focus on one subject at a time as well as the habits of diligence, order, and punctuality, I have made significant accomplishments.*
>
> — *Moustafa Kadous*

Being late to an appointment is similar to breaking a promise, and it can cost you the trust of other persons. It's also proof that you lack self-discipline and organizational skills.

Create a new challenge of self-discipline for yourself. Start by getting to every appointment at least five minutes early. After one month, this habit should become your new normal.

Adopt Lifelong Learning | 354

> *Lifelong learning is no longer a luxury but a necessity for employment.*

Jay Samit

Reflect on what you envision for your future; lifelong learning should be about you and not about other people. Explore specific areas of interest where you want to make improvements. Research and read about your interests; it will give you an idea of how you can get started with your learning. Also, plan out how the requirements of how your new learning will fit into your life. If it doesn't fit now, develop a plan for what you need to do to make it suitable.

355 | Consistent Improvement

> *Continuous improvement is better than delayed perfection.*
>
> *Mark Twain*

After learning to live the self-disciplined life, you need to consistently strengthen it. Otherwise, you will lose it. You need to set new challenges and reject instant gratification in favor of bigger future rewards.

There's no such thing as being disciplined enough. There will always be an area where you need to make improvements or expand your comfort zone.

With such consistent practice, you will maintain your best levels and bring out the better version of your best levels.

Replace Bad Habits with Good Ones | 356

> *A nail is driven out by another nail. Habit is overcome by habit.*

Desiderius Erasmus

Awareness is the first step to breaking bad habits.

Stress and boredom are the two main causes of bad habits. Track the number of times your bad habit happens per day. Anytime your bad habit manifests, mark it down on your paper. Then, count the tally marks at the end of the day.

The goal is not to judge yourself; it is to become aware of the frequency at which it happens.

Keep in mind that you need time, effort, and perseverance to break bad habits.

357 | Make Continuous Effort

> *Continuous Effort - not strength or intelligence - is the key to unlocking our potential.*
>
> Winston Churchill

Consistent efforts lead to lasting fulfillment, achievement, and success. You will only have the illusion of success through occasional effort.

When you repeat small, unassuming efforts with consistency, it will lead to a never-ending stream of value.

Keep giving your best effort to your life and your world; then, you will be on your path to accomplishing your most treasured dreams.

Something Else | 358

> *Success seems to be largely a matter of hanging on after others have let go.*

William Feather

After you've used up all your existing options, get creative, and create more options. There's always another step you can take to keep going. Be curious enough and persistent enough to experiment and adjust what no longer works until you get the job done.

You have the option to give more; don't give up. Believe in your abilities and maximize those abilities to create new options, keep going, and achieve the success you desire.

359 | Broaden Your Horizons

> The joy of life comes from our encounters with new experiences and hence, there is no greater joy than having an endlessly changing horizon, for each day to have a new and different sun.

Christopher McCandless

A fantastic way to become more successful and more educated person is to expose yourself to various disciplines and expand your knowledge.

For example, you can find powerful life lessons from industries and professions that have nothing to do with personal development. Start today by being inquisitive about knowledge in other fields.

Address the Real Mistakes | 360

> *Your best teacher is your last mistake.*

Ralph Nader

You're being unfair to yourself when you proclaim that you are worthless because you made one mistake. Also, it is highly likely that you will develop learned helplessness and even deny yourself the opportunity to improve.

Here's what you should do: identify actions you took that failed to generate your desired outcome. That way, you'll address the mistake and not criticize yourself wrongly.

361 | Cognitive Reframing

> ...inverse paranoia is the most outwardly identifiable quality of a high-performing person.
>
> *Brian Tracy*

Cognitive reframing is the process of giving a positive slant to the meaning of difficulty, failure, or hardship. Develop "inverse paranoia." It's a belief that everything that happens to you will lead you to success and that the world conspires to do you good.

End Bad Relationships for Good | 362

> *Find the person who is more interested in making a positive impact in your life than just changing your relationship status.*

Moustafa Kadous

Are you more miserable than happy in a current relationship? Here are some proven ways to end such relationships for good:

- Decide once and for all that you are going to end it. Be so convinced that nothing or anybody can change your mind.

- Think of positive ways to spend the free time you have after the breakup. Examples; join a gym, do volunteer work, or take a class. Meeting with new folks will improve your mood.

363 | Old Habits

> *Breaking old habits and forming new ones always take time, but it is worth it in the end.*
>
> *Joyce Meyer*

If you keep repeating your routine all the days of your life, nothing new will come into your life to change it. Opening new doors means trying new things to allow new opportunities to flow into your life.

Take five minutes every day to use words in describing your current old habits and aspirational new habits. Observe the results after four weeks, and you will be surprised by the quality of change you will have made.

Don't Be Scared to Be the One-Minute Fool | 364

> *Asking questions makes you seem foolish only for a moment. But if you don't ask questions, you'll never know, and you might lose lots of benefits for that lack of knowledge.*

Moustafa Kadous

Are you afraid to ask questions because you don't want to look foolish or stupid? The truth is, if you don't say anything or ask questions, you'll never learn what you ought to know. Though you might receive some flak for asking, the sting will wear off soon. You would have only been a fool for a minute and not for the rest of your life.

Do you want to be a fool for one minute or a fool forever? The choice is yours, but make a wise choice.

Always ask any question you wish to know whether they are about the fundamentals of the discussion, an application, or a specific part of the discussion. Seek understanding.

365 | Knowledge Is Power

> *Knowledge is power. Information is liberating. Education is the premise of progress, in every society, in every family.*

Kofi Annan

There will always be something to be known. Every day is an opportunity to discover something new.

Knowledge increases when you share it. It illuminates an accessible and workable path to your goal. It even provides you with the tools you need to build that path.

Start acting on your knowledge; you will experience vast improvement for the rest of your life.

YOUR JOURNEY CONTINUES...

You've been discovering how to unlock your best self. But your journey isn't over. Just knowing how to be your best doesn't make you your best. You need to take action on all you have learned. That means do it: practice the new habits and strategies, correct your path when you stray, and reward yourself for progress every day.

I encourage you to go back through each of the 365 messages regularly to reinforce your "best you" for life. Share these inspirations and tips with your family, friends, and colleagues, and pay it forward. I invite you to the KadouScope (K-Forum) community to share your stories, your favorite inspirations, and your tips to help others unlock the best they can be.
www.kadouscope.com/k-forum

I celebrate your journey, your dreams, and you.

About the Author

Moustafa Kadous is a leading transformational entrepreneur, dynamic personal life and business coach and public speaker. Believing that learning is a lifetime pursuit, Moustafa has passionately pursued knowledge, wisdom, and skills throughout his life. From his time as an impoverished youth through his young adult skirmishes and successive business ventures that have shaped his destiny, Moustafa has gained global recognition as a business leader and architect of many successful companies.

Across the past fifteen years, Moustafa created multiple enterprises from scratch, turning each into profitable multi-million-dollar revenue generators. His life's work is carried forward through his company, Skilled Now, a global conglomerate of businesses spread across the globe. His diverse portfolio includes technology solutions, business and soft skills training, business process outsourcing, career training and certification, and professional online coaching services. The common thread is his mission to enable individuals, businesses, and nations to maximize their possibilities and do so through leading-edge technology and practical business solutions. The goal is worldwide economic prosperity. He manages these businesses through offices in the United States, Portugal, Saudi Arabia, UAE, and Egypt.